KNOW YOUR WHY

FINDING AND FULFILLING YOUR CALLING IN LIFE

KEN COSTA

W PUBLISHING GROUP

AN IMPRINT OF THOMAS NELSON

Published in Nashville, Tennessee, by W Publishing, an imprint of Thomas Nelson.

Thomas Nelson titles may be purchased in bulk for educational, business, fund-raising, or sales promotional use. For information, please e-mail SpecialMarkets@ThomasNelson.com.

Unless otherwise noted, Scripture quotations are taken from the Holy Bible, New International Version', NIV'. Copyright © 1973, 1978, 1984, 2011 by Biblica, Inc.' Used by permission of Zondervan. All rights reserved worldwide. www.zondervan.com. The "NIV" and "New International Version" are trademarks registered in the United States Patent and Trademark Office by Biblica, Inc.'

Scripture quotations marked AMP are from the Amplified' Bible. Copyright © 1954, 1958, 1962, 1964, 1965, 1987 by The Lockman Foundation. Used by permission. (www.Lockman.org)

Scripture quotations marked GNT are from the Good News Translation in Today's English Version—Second Edition. Copyright 1992 by American Bible Society. Used by permission.

Scripture quotations marked THE MESSAGE are from The Message. Copyright © by Eugene H. Peterson 1993, 1994, 1995, 1996, 2000, 2001, 2002. Used by permission of Tyndale House Publishers, Inc.

Scripture quotations marked NKJV are from the New King James Version'. © 1982 by Thomas Nelson. Used by permission. All rights reserved.

To preserve anonymity, names and occupations have been changed.

ISBN 978-0-7180-8771-5 (SC)
ISBN 978-0-7180-8774-6 (eBook)

Library of Congress Cataloging-in-Publication Data

Library of Congress Control Number: 2016933595

Printed in the United States of America

17 18 19 20 RRD 10 9 8 7 6

*I dedicate this book to my wife, Fi. This book would have
been impossible without her constant love and support.
We journey together to find our life-callings.
And to Georgina, Nick, Charles, Henry, Jenny, and Claudia,
who never hesitate to challenge and always encourage me.
And to my late mother, Martha Faith, who prayed.*

Contents

FOREWORD

IT IS ESTIMATED THE AVERAGE PERSON WILL SPEND 150,000 hours at work in his or her lifetime. That translates to roughly 40 percent of our lives being spent at work. That's a lot. As a result, our work, our jobs, and how we spend the majority of our time are very important to God. And, as it turns out, throughout the Bible God has a lot to say about our work. Yet many of the people I meet are either dissatisfied with their work or don't feel like they are in the right jobs. They are unsure whether they have been specifically called by God. This is an important issue, one that deserves time exploring.

That's why I can't think of anyone more qualified to write about the significance of knowing your purpose than my friend Ken Costa. I first met Ken in Davos, Switzerland, at the World Economic Forum, where we were both speakers. Ken's forty years of high-level experience as an investment banker in international finance make him a voice worth listening to when it comes to the global economy. And, as the long-time chairman of Alpha Ministries, Ken also has proven his heart for God and his people. Ken's life is a beautiful example of what can happen when we embrace God's purpose in the workplace. That is why I was very happy to endorse his first book, *God at Work*.

His new book, *Know Your Why: Finding and Fulfilling Your Calling in Life*, is absolutely foundational to living a purpose driven life. Calling is the pivot of a fulfilled Christian life. You see, God has decided that we should all engage in work. It's not a bad thing or something we should dread. Most of us work in order to meet our basic needs; we have a responsibility toward our families, and we have bills to pay. And the Bible supports this. From beginning to end, the Bible addresses how men and women should and should not approach work.

Yet God has also placed in each of us a longing for meaning. We know there is more to life, and so we search for fulfillment and work that seems worthwhile. Which leads us to a larger discussion about calling and gifts and talents. How can we use the talents we have to help others and glorify God? This is particularly true of those in their twenties and thirties, who have grown up in a multichoice world, which, for all its freedom, has created real uncertainty in people's life callings.

Ken understands that Jesus cares deeply about our daily work. Not only that, but Jesus has uniquely gifted each one of us to make a distinct contribution. No two people are alike, and we all need each other to function. The same is true of our callings at work; each person brings something uniquely different to the task at hand.

Then why do so many people struggle to find their places in life? Many people cannot see past a difficult boss or unemployment or a stagnant job. And when it comes to incorporating faith at work and deriving some sort of calling out of it, there can be an even larger disconnect. If you have wrestled with these questions, I invite you to closely read the pages that follow. In them, Ken Costa unwraps some of the basic ways we can begin this journey of discovery. It's practical and life shaping, distilled from forty years of wrestling with these issues in the workplace.

Ken asserts—and I agree—that God first wants us to know that he *loves* us, that we are *known* to him, and that, yes, he has *called* us. This basic reassurance—the idea of being loved, known, and called—is found throughout the Bible and is just as vital today as it was back then. Ken unpacks each of these ideas in *Know Your Why*. Knowing that the Lord begins by approaching his people with tremendous love adds a real layer of comfort to Ken's teaching.

This is not what the world tells us, however. The world's system will encourage us to strive on our own and become the masters of our own fates. Yet what I have seen over and over again is that you can be the most talented person, have the best connections with influential people, have plenty of money at your disposal, and still not be effective or fulfilled. Why is that?

Well, Jesus told us plainly in John's gospel when he said, "I am the vine; you are the branches. If you remain in me and I in you, you will bear much fruit; apart from me you can do nothing" (John 15:5 NIV). The longer I live, the more I have found that statement to be true. When we allow God to be the source of our decisions in life, we have found the basis of our callings.

If you're looking for a self-help book to help you become famous and make a lot of money, this is not the book for you. On the other hand, if you are serious about seeking your calling in work and in life, I wholeheartedly suggest you listen to what Ken Costa has to say. Searching after your why will require a good amount of faith and risk. It may even be uncomfortable for a while. However, if you trust the One who is calling, he will be sure to help you on your journey.

One other thing before I let you go: Ken has one of the best British accents I've ever heard. So as you read, I sincerely hope you hear these words as if spoken by a classically trained British actor. It makes the journey that much more enjoyable.

—PASTOR RICK WARREN

INTRODUCTION

THIS IS A BOOK ABOUT A QUESTION. IT'S A QUESTION I'VE asked myself a thousand times in a thousand different ways. A question that has kept me motivated during the workday and often kept me awake during sleepless nights. It's the question most frequently asked of me by those seasoned in their faith, but also by those just beginning their Christian walks, and I've no doubt it's a question that you have asked just as frequently. It's a hopeful question and a searching question. A question that goes right to the heart of our sense of being and belonging in the world.

Why am I here?

And not just here on earth. *Why am I here in this city? Why am I here in this job, this church, this club, this group? Why am I here?*

Wrapped up in this question are so many others—*Where should I be going? What should I be doing? How should I be living my life?*—all of them fundamentally linked to the search for purpose and direction that has characterized much of my adult life. As a teenager, growing up in apartheid South Africa; as a student at Cambridge University; as a young man starting out in the City of London and later as an experienced financial advisor; as the chairman of various charities and church initiatives, but also as a husband and father and friend—so much of my life has been a response to that question.

This isn't an existential question, cried out to the empty air with no hope of reply. Instead, it's a directed question, one I've asked in expectation of an answer.

It's a question I've been asking and continue to ask of God.

You see, at the heart of the Christian faith is a big, fat *why*. And that *why* takes the shape of a calling. A calling for us to be *here*, in this place and at this time. A calling for us to live out our faith and values in the rough-and-tumble of our everyday existence. A calling to engage with the world around us in the power and the light of Christ.

The content of that calling—of that *why*—is set out in the Bible. It's the Great Commandment of Christ, to "love the Lord your God with all your heart and with all your soul and with all your strength and with all your mind" and to "love your neighbor as yourself" (Luke 10:27). It's the Great Commission, to "go and make disciples of all nations" (Matthew 28:19). Or the great call to compassion that the book of Micah describes so beautifully: "What does the LORD require of you? To act justly and to love mercy and to walk humbly with your God" (Micah 6:8).

The difficulty is working out how to follow that call. This common calling that applies to every Christian in every age and in every walk of life—to make known the good news of Christ to every generation—is unchanged by circumstance or culture. So what does that look like practically, for each of us as individuals, in our own unique situations? What does the Great Commission have to say specifically to you and me at seven forty-five on a Monday morning, in a traffic jam or crammed into a commuter train, on the way back to work? What does it mean for someone to act justly and love mercy while serving coffee to strangers all day? One of the great struggles of modern faith, I believe, is trying to work out what our common calling looks like in the here and now.

For many years now, I've had the great privilege of mentoring men and women, often in their twenties and thirties. And these questions have confronted me more than any other: *What does that*

Christian calling look like for me? *How can I even begin to understand it or put it into practice? How could I ever play a part in God's great story?*

How can I come to know my why?

It can be difficult to imagine that God wants to call us individually, with all our frailties and brokenness, to be his hands and feet in this needy world. The world seems so big, the problems so vast, and we can feel so insignificant. But I believe that this process of seeing the plans and purposes to which God might put us, is the great adventure of faith. As Paul put it in his letter to the Ephesians, "we are God's handiwork, created in Christ Jesus to do good works, which God prepared in advance for us to do" (Ephesians 2:10).

This book is the fruit of countless conversations and reflections through which I have tried to work out—for myself and for others—what it might look like to follow Christ's calling in the here and now. What it might look like in practice to live out a life of everyday engagement with this everyday God. As you read, it is my hope that you will allow God to draw out your passions and hopes, your dreams and desires; that you will nurture them, grow them, build on them, and then use them to shape your life and the lives of those around you in ways you never thought possible. Be assured of this: whoever you are and wherever you are, God has great plans for you. That is part of what makes the Christian life so compelling, so hopeful, and so exciting.

Our callings matter. I am passionate about helping others find true, fulfilling causes to live for. We will only be able to do this by believing that *we are called with a purpose, both individually and as a community.* We must believe that God has a plan, and this plan involves *us.* Jesus taught that we are not on earth by accident but by a clear intention of God, for lives to be lived well and in tune with God's desires.

To even begin that journey, we need to be convinced that these callings can be lived out in a practical way. This is not some personal pietistic enclosure of the righteous but the wider call to engagement in the community around us.

Yet understanding what our callings might look like is even harder for this generation than for any previous one. We live in a multichoice world. We all face questions about where our talents and passions might be best put to use. The pressures are enormous precisely because the choices are so wide-open and often confusing. The speed of change is frightening, and yet the opportunity to be challenged and stimulated has never been greater.

Since my faith came alive over forty years ago, I have lived out this calling of Christ as best I can. Sometimes I've taken a wrong turn. Sometimes I've faced difficult choices of my own. And sometimes I've felt clearly the voice of Christ at my elbow, pushing me to take a certain route.

Of course, when that voice does break through, it is life-transforming. One of the most significant moments in my Christian life occurred when, as a young man, I took some time to be alone, to pray, and to seek the Lord. I was walking along the river Thames in London, not long after I had started working in the City—the name given to London's financial district. I was feeling deeply despondent, and that question—*Why am I here?*—was in the forefront of my mind. I felt a lack of purpose and direction, and I couldn't see how my work could possibly fit into God's plans. Surely full-time ministry would be closer to God's purposes for me. The cutthroat competition of the market-driven economy seemed so far removed from the values of the kingdom.

But then, as clearly and as suddenly as a dolphin breaking through the surface of the sea, Luke 24:49 burst into my head. "*Stay in the city until you have been clothed with power from on high.*" It came from nowhere, and I knew instantly it was a word from God. It was an answer from Scripture—used in a different context, but powerful in its resonance of truth. So I stayed in the City. And through my staying God has opened up incredible opportunities for me to shine something of his light in that place. When God shows us his purposes for our lives, he also gives us the power through his Spirit to fulfill these purposes.

The point is that God comes alongside us in our callings. He works with us in relationship. Clearly God sometimes breaks into our lives in a big way, just as he did to mine while I walked along the Thames. But other times it is much gentler—a beckoning and a whispering. Sometimes God places roadblocks if we are going in the wrong direction. And sometimes it may well be up to us to decide the way ahead. Whatever the circumstances, we have a God who walks beside us, helping us keep a sure footing when the path ahead seems uncertain.

Your calling is the deep inner conviction of the Holy Spirit that the whole of your life matters to God—both where you have come from and where you are going. If you take nothing else from this book, know that God loves you more than you can imagine. He knows you better than you know yourself. And out of that place of love and knowledge, he has called you into the world to change the world with his marvelous light. You are uniquely loved, known, and called by God. This is the bedrock of your security in the world.

"You did not choose me, but I chose you and appointed you so that you might go and bear fruit—fruit that will last" (John 15:16). So it was with the first disciples, and so it is with us. It is Jesus who chooses us; we do not choose him. He gives us a clear purpose—that we might bear fruit. No life-calling from Jesus is barren. This fruit-bearing is not a one-off spiritual high, not a temporary fix, but the development of a fruit that will last. It produces the sustainable fruit of the Spirit that matures each day throughout our lives.

Remember that you will never again have these days, these relationships, these circumstances, these God-given opportunities. Making the most of life and enjoying it to the full are the challenges and promises of Jesus.

I want to finish with two Bible passages that persuaded me to write this book.

The first was a word that came to me in a moment of real darkness, at a time when I felt hopelessly lost. All of us can go through such times of intense difficulty when our spiritual lives are hard and a kind of "dark night of the soul" comes upon us. Joy becomes forced rather than flowing naturally. Turbulence, rather than peace, is the reigning emotion. It can seem as if little will help.

In this moment of darkness, a verse from Luke leapt out at me: "Simon, Simon, Satan has asked to sift all of you as wheat. But I have prayed for you, Simon, that your faith may not fail. And when you have turned back, strengthen your brothers" (Luke 22:31–32).

This was an obscure passage, and I struggled at first to understand its significance. But as I read it through again, I was drawn to that last sentence: "When you have turned back, strengthen your brothers."

As Christians, we inevitably go through times when we feel lost, as if we are drifting along without any real purpose. We experience times of doubt, times of "sifting," when we struggle to trust that God really is in control or that he has a plan for our lives. Since that moment I have longed to strengthen those who try to make the very best of their lives. Like me, they have been sifted and spiritually assaulted, but Christ intercedes on our behalf, praying that our faith holds true. And as we come through that sifting, it is Christ who becomes the cornerstone on which lives are rebuilt, careers changed, hopes fulfilled, and new depths of maturity discovered.

The second passage of Scripture that motivated me to write this book was one I found while praying aloud at a retreat for young leaders, in the shadow of Windsor Castle. In a moment of quiet reflection, I found myself quoting the words of Psalm 71: "Even when I am old and gray, do not forsake me, my God, till I declare your power to the next generation, your mighty acts to all who are to come" (v. 18).

Over the years, that verse has come to signify the heart of what I feel God has called me to. It has fueled within me the desire not only to strengthen my generation to find in Christ their cornerstone, but to remind the *next* generation of the mighty acts of God. For many years, that has been my great passion—a central aspect of my calling and my purpose.

May I challenge you, then, to think about your passions and your purposes as you read through this book. Don't give in to the lie that you are too insignificant for God to have a plan for your life, but listen for his "gentle whisper" (1 Kings 19:12). God has called you by name. He makes straight the roads and makes clear the paths, if only you let him.

Purpose matters. I hope this book will help you find yours.

ONE

CALLED TO PASSION

"WHAT DO YOU WANT?"

These are the first words Jesus spoke in John's gospel (John 1:38).

What are you really looking for? What lifts you to a new level? What makes you want to get out of bed on a winter's day, grab hold of the day, and make the most of every moment? What is it that gives meaning to your life? What enables you to navigate the confusion of a world that changes every nanosecond? Which values make every day worth living in a world that seems hostile to the good news of Jesus?

These are all questions that can be answered if we grasp the driving importance of Jesus' first question: *What do you really want?* And this question is addressed to all of us.

But I hear echoing back at me, *Surely this can't be right. It sounds selfish. What I want surely doesn't matter. It's what Jesus wants that's important. And anyway, isn't this a superficial question? The answers that immediately spring to mind certainly seem to be: a pay raise, a new car, a nice vacation, the latest gadgets.*

No. The question Jesus asked is profound. It goes beyond the material wish list. It confronts us and forces us to think seriously about our true longings and objectives. Perhaps that is why these are the first spoken words of Jesus that John recorded in his gospel.

Mark's gospel recorded another instance, when blind Bartimaeus called out to Jesus, "Son of David, have mercy on me!" (Mark 10:48). And again, Jesus asked him, "What do you want me to do for you?" (v. 51). Jesus knew exactly what this blind man wanted, but he asked the question so that Bartimaeus himself would articulate directly to Jesus exactly what he was longing for: "Rabbi, I want to see" (v. 51). It matters to Jesus what the desires of our hearts are.

And that is why Jesus' question is so powerful. It forces us to search deeply into our motives for what *really* drives us to live every day with purpose.

The disciples were not dissimilar from us: they were seekers, trying to make sense of their purposes. And that first encounter with Jesus, recorded in John's gospel, is riveting.

Here were two disciples who had been in the desert with John the Baptist, who was preaching a gospel of repentance in expectation of the Messiah. John was a celebrity, a life coach, a guru. His message was one of self-help and self-improvement—a message of repentance from sin that could not yet rely on the power of the Spirit to be sustained. People from Jerusalem and the surrounding towns flocked to hear him. They wanted answers about how to live with a real and defined purpose, answers not only for themselves but also for the nation of Israel as a whole. But there was something unfulfilled in their lives that could not be satisfied by John's teaching, radical and appealing as it was. They were going to John for a self-help fix, but nobody realized better than John that self-help could only go so far. Then the disciples saw Jesus:

> When [John] saw Jesus passing by, he said, "Look, the Lamb of God!"
>
> When the two disciples heard him say this, they followed Jesus. Turning around, Jesus saw them following and asked, "What do you want?" (John 1:36–38)

The action started with Jesus. He broke into *their* world as he passed by them. It was not they who had to seek him out. All they had to do was be ready and waiting when he came—ready to take the risk and follow where he led. The disciples knew something was missing, and they saw in this encounter with Jesus something of what they had hoped for. The rest was up to Jesus. And he did not disappoint—as he never disappoints those who genuinely want to hear his call.

And so the disciples turned to follow Jesus. They said nothing. They must have been bursting with questions. Shouldn't the disciples have asked him the burning question that their search for truth with John the Baptist had been all about: "Are you the one who is to be revealed as Savior of oppressed Israel?" But they didn't. They just followed him. There was something about him that drew them in. Something intangible and inexplicable. They saw in Jesus something more than repentance. They saw the missing piece of their lives—a relationship with God himself.

And then Jesus turned to face them.

I cannot get the image of Jesus turning around out of my mind. It is so much part of my life. How many times have I faced the big issues—choosing a career, proposing to my wife, changing jobs, dealing with conflict at work and in relationships—and chosen to follow his guidance? Yet, how often have I done so and not quite believed he would notice I was following? In my mind, a follower is the one who looks mostly at the leader's back. But Jesus turns *toward* his followers. In the culture of the time, this was a profound sign of acknowledgment and recognition. He noticed them. Their anonymity disappeared.

He doesn't merely stride on purposefully as some leaders might do, expecting their followers to tag along behind. In the simple act of turning he shows his regard for every one of us seeking our callings. Attention is God's greatest gift to us. He reaches out to us, and he responds as if we were the only ones marked for special attention.

Such is his love for us. A well-known saying observes, "Don't walk in front of me; I may not follow. Don't walk behind me; I may not lead. Just walk beside me and be my friend." And likewise, Jesus said to his disciples, "I have called you friends" (John 15:15).

Jesus' question to the disciples goes more than skin deep. The word we translate as "want" is the Greek word *zeteo*, which means "to seek." So the question "What do you want?" is not a dismissive "What are you after?" It's not a confused "Why are you following me?" Rather, Jesus is asking the deeper question of "What are you seeking?"

The drift of Jesus' question is clear. What is the principal desire in your life? What are your passions? What dreams do you long to see fulfilled? What makes your life worth living? In effect, what is the main driver of your life, your calling?

FINDING YOUR PASSION

All of this talk about your passions, your dreams, your desires might seem selfish and confusing. I first met Rick Warren when we were both speaking at the World Economic Forum in Switzerland. Looking around at the titans of industry and politics, I remember him saying, "We must always be mindful that *it's not about you*." This then became the opening sentence and most quoted remark of his book *The Purpose Driven Life*.[1] In many ways this is a life-transforming truism, a huge challenge to the self-driven life. It's a reminder that to be a follower of Christ is to live for others; that your purpose cannot be fulfilled outside of the community of God's people. That's why church, the gathering of the local people of God, is so vital in helping you find your true calling.

But on another level, what *you* want is so important. Your passions and dreams are the fuels that feed the fire of God's calling. God really is interested in you. He really is interested in what it is that makes you tick. He really does call you, just as you are.

Very often when people talk about calling, they try to remove human autonomy from the equation. They imagine that our desires, our concerns, our passions and talents are irrelevant. But the fact that our loving Father has called us should not negate the freedom we have to make choices. There is nothing in Christian faith to encourage the resigned acceptance of fate. *Que sera, sera*— "whatever will be, will be"—might be an old favorite song, but it is not the basis of our callings. Something much more liberating, exciting, and fulfilling lies ahead when we seriously seek the call of God in our lives.

Following his call isn't about blind obedience. It's more like leaving a house with a friend to go on a journey. You both have a shared destination in mind and a map to get you there, but there are many routes you could take along the way. And so you work out your route in conversation and relationship. Sometimes your friend might suggest very strongly that you both take a certain path. Perhaps she knows something about the way ahead that you don't. Sometimes you might insist on taking a wrong turn, away from the destination, and have to allow your friend to show you the right direction. But you work it out together. That is what I believe it means to follow your calling with Christ. *Your* opinions, *your* passions, *your* desires really do matter to him.

This is something we see very clearly in the Bible—particularly in the journeys of Saint Paul. The letters of Paul paint a picture of a man who was constantly probing at different doors, trying to work out in dialogue with God where his next steps might go. There's no sense that his path was laid out clearly before him. Sometimes his attempts to take a certain road were blocked by forces outside of his control, and sometimes he was responding to a very specific message of the Holy Spirit. But very often, Paul simply followed his nose, listening to his own heart while keeping himself open to the promptings of the Spirit of God.

The point is, we are not called to be robots. God does not

dictate our paths but gives us wide room to maneuver. So often I hear people say that if they make a wrong choice they have missed their call. But often it is not the presenting decision but the purposeful direction that matters. After all, it was God who gave us our unique humanity—who put those passions and talents within us, for us to use.

Crucial to understanding our callings, then, is understanding ourselves. Seeing the passions and desires that God has placed within us—the talents and dreams that await realization in him.

The truth is that God gives us passions for a reason. He will not call us into something that makes us miserable or that is a waste of our talents. Frederick Buechner, the American theologian, once wrote, "The place God calls you to is the place where your deep gladness and the world's deep hunger meet."[2] The fact that we are passionate about something is often a sign that this is where God is calling us to be.

Of course, some needs are more conspicuous than others, and some passions can strike us as more obviously worthy than others. When I was growing up in South Africa under the brutal apartheid regime, my fellow students and I deeply desired to see that iniquitous system broken once and for all. We had a cause that was clear-cut, single-minded, and driven by a commitment to justice—an unequivocal calling. We believed in it. Many were prepared to die for it, and some of my fellow students did just that. We never doubted that in the end our case for justice would prevail. And so the student movement at the time committed itself to undermining the regime as best we could.

It can seem more difficult to find a cause worth fighting for, let alone dying for, in this modern, noncommittal world where anything seems to go. Yet we can see many remaining injustices, if we take the time to look. The trafficking of people as sex slaves, the destruction of parts of the planet, the scourge of extreme poverty, and the growth of inequality at our own back doors are but a few pressing examples of injustices crying out for the transforming hope of the gospel. As I write this book, millions of refugees are fleeing battle-scarred countries such as Syria and Libya, hoping to start new lives in Europe.

But it's also important to remember that the world's deep hunger for Jesus is not confined to deprived communities and instances of injustice in war-torn areas of the world. Anyone who has ever worked on a bank trading floor knows the spiritual emptiness that can accompany the cutthroat competition and false bravado on show there. That is a place of deep hunger, and that same hunger exists throughout the working world. The world is hungry for godly lawyers, godly bankers, godly charity workers, godly shop assistants, and godly teachers! The great and humbling truth of Christianity is that God in his wisdom chooses to work *through* us and *with* us. He calls us out to be his hands and feet in the world, each with a special role to play in the expansion of his kingdom.

Finding our passions—answering the question "What do you want?"—is therefore crucial to finding our callings. Rarely is that question easily answered. For most, determining what we truly want is a profound psychological process: a journey of discovery that takes time to travel and that can lead us in different directions at different points in our lives. What I most wanted as a graduate entering the job market was different from what I wanted when I first got married. I faced my deepest longings in different ways at different times. That is why the pursuit of our callings is something that permeates every moment of our lives.

So it was for the disciples. They didn't know what they wanted—only that they were searching for *something*. When Jesus asked them, "What do you want?" they didn't know how to answer. Instead they sidestepped it with a question of their own: "Where are you staying?" (John 1:38).

The inference from the disciples' question is clear: *We don't know the answer to your question. We're not sure what we're seeking.*

We don't know where we're going. But we do know that we want to spend time with you, to abide with you, to learn more about you. Because if you truly are who John says you are, then maybe you will be able to show us what we are truly seeking.

In this simple exchange we have a most powerful link to our generation. Confronted with so many options and possibilities at our fingertips with unlimited knowledge just a Google search away, how many of us struggle to work out what we truly want? How many of us recognize that there is something missing, without understanding what it could be? But Jesus knows the longings of this generation so well. He isn't critical of our failure to answer the question that he poses, just as he wasn't critical of the disciples. Instead, he responds to us as he did to the disciples: "Come and you will see" (v. 39).

Jesus' simple response to the disciples also acknowledged their unspoken questions. The words, "Come and see where I am staying," meant, "Come and find out the plans that I have for you; the callings and the passions that I will give you." And that is exactly what the disciples did. They entered the house seeking—but they left sought. For Jesus sought them out and called them. They gave up their searches for truth and took up new callings and new identities, not because *they* had all the answers, but because they found the one who does. They found not a new religious project, not a new program, but a *person*. They became known to him, and that recognition changed their lives.

Andrew lost no time. He knew that this was the Messiah, and he responded, grabbing hold of his brother Simon and introducing him to Jesus. Jesus recognized Simon immediately and renamed him—he was to be called the rock: "Jesus looked at him and said, 'You are Simon son of John. You will be called Cephas' (which, when translated, is Peter [rock])" (v. 42).

This is breathtaking authority. Can you imagine interviewing someone for a job and the first thing you do is change her name?

"You were known as Philippa in your previous job, but in this place you will be known as Jane."

It is interesting to note that, in the Gospels, Simon (Peter) was anything but a rock; he was impulsive and unstable. But in Acts, he was the pillar of the early church. Jesus named him not for what he was but for what, by God's grace, he was to *become*. Jesus knew Simon's future as well as his past.

And so it is with us as we struggle to find our true callings. Jesus reaches toward us. He does the calling, seeing us not as we have been pigeonholed by our own and others' definitions, but by what he, through his indwelling Holy Spirit in our lives, is shaping us to be. Our lives are meaningful, not because we fulfill the *projections* of others but because we follow the *promises* of God for our future well-beings.

In the next few verses of John's account, we see the calling of the first disciples.

From one encounter, Philip joined up. Nathaniel had sneered at the name of Nazareth and had asked whether any good could come from it, and yet he joined up immediately, once Jesus had revealed that he knew where Nathaniel had been even before Philip called him. The attraction of Jesus and the power of his personality went viral. In these few verses, we see a first-century social network.

When truth takes hold of an individual, it does so with such overwhelming conviction that others need to be told.

In my experience, when I take hold of the words of Jesus, his words take hold of me. Jesus' words, "You call me 'Teacher' and 'Lord,' and rightly so, for that is what I am" (John 13:13), transformed my life when I first read them as a student, and they continue to transform me now. Jesus calls with all the commanding firmness of the Lord who is accustomed to being followed, and yet with the gentle compassion of the teacher who is longing to draw alongside his pupil. Jesus' words are powerful to change our lives. That is why the fact that he asks, "What do you want?" is of vital, immediate, compelling importance. It's not that the answer to the question becomes clear, but that the *source* of that answer is revealed. His question is not simply an inquiry but an offer. Jesus offers us the chance to join in a relationship with him through which we will find out what he is calling us to.

I know how long it took me to understand—and I do so only partially even now—that Jesus asks this question directly to each one of us, today, in whatever our situations may be. But we cannot answer him from the pressure and stress of the working environment any more than the disciples could answer from the heat of the desert. A response requires time with Jesus. The disciples went off to hang out with him away from the feverish world of the crowds. We need to do the same, never more so than in our 24/7, "always on" world.

I recall sitting with my immediate boss in a lunchroom overlooking London Bridge. I was working for one of the leading global financial institutions as the deal maker for new transactions. It was that time of the year so many of us love and hate: the end-of-year performance review.

I looked across the City of London, imagining the centuries of trade and commercial activity that had taken place in what is still the greatest financial center in the world. I remembered that the coat of arms of the City—*Domine dirige nos* ("Lord guide us")—tells the story of a history of dependence on God. The merchants and bankers, the coffee traders and gold dealers, the insurance companies and guilds of the past all had sought God's guidance.

My boss asked me what my objectives were, what I was expecting to achieve, and what I wanted out of life and my job. I said that what I really wanted to do with my life was to make Jesus Christ known to our generation. Ultimately that was what motivated me: to seek his guidance on all aspects of my day-to-day banking work, just as the City fathers, dealers, and merchants had over the centuries. My boss could not have looked more confused and stuck for words, partly because we were doing a compensation review and the idea of mixing God and money unsettled him. He wanted to deal with my past performance, the bank's current objectives, and my prospects for the next year. Of course, I was also ready for that discussion and was well versed in the arguments for why my achievements of the last year should be properly rewarded. But I couldn't help but respond authentically to his question, "What do you want?"

Very often, when Jesus asks that question, we have no idea what the exact answer is. But our immediate response should nevertheless be, *I want to hang out with you. I want to find out more about you. I want to be regarded as part of the family that meets in your home, in exactly the same way as the invitation was extended to those two disciples. Because I know that in hanging out with you and getting to know you, what I truly want for my life will become clear.*

John used the word *meno* thirty-three times in his gospel. You can see why this word was so important to him when you understand its meaning: the English translation is "abiding with," "staying connected," and "resting in." Indeed, the key to making the best of your life, the key to discovering your calling, is *to be with* Jesus. As you stay with Jesus, you find out more about what he has in store for you. He knows your passions, your fears, and the deepest desires of your heart. As with Peter, Jesus knows your name. As with Nathaniel, he knows your nature. As with Philip, he knows your uncertainty.

Jesus knows who we are. But he also knows who we are becoming. He has a vested interest in seeing us flourish in the future. One of the great joys of reading through the New Testament is seeing how these flawed, fallible, and lost disciples grew into their callings, transforming from wandering fishermen into the founders of the early church through the empowering presence of Jesus and the Holy Spirit. And it all started with that first question, that first encounter: "What do you want?"

The disciples didn't have an answer. They grew to know that

answer over many years, as they discovered more about themselves, more about their hearts, and more about the amazing plans God had in store for them. As they discovered more about what it meant to build this new, revolutionary kingdom of God, they came to understand more about where God was calling them.

We do not need to answer Jesus immediately, but we do need to draw close to him. For as he shows us more about ourselves, we learn more about the powerful calling he has on our lives, callings that equip us to see a future where the best is yet to come.

So often the world expects you to behave in a certain way. Perhaps your parents wanted you to join the family business or teachers encouraged you to study one subject or another. But often what the world has planned for you and what God has planned for you are very different.

One of my favorite worship songs, written by Will Reagan of United Pursuit, is called "Help Me Find My Own Flame." The central theme is that we cannot simply rely on the passions of others; instead we need to find our own flames. It captures perfectly the idea that we have unique identities, and that we should not compete with or compare ourselves to one another.

We cannot make the most of life and live well if we are trying to be someone else. God is not interested in calling clones. He invests in you and me as individuals. We each have a unique mold, customized in Christ for perfection. He wants us to be passionate, sold out to do the specific tasks that he has prepared for us. He enlarges our often-narrow visions of what we can achieve in our lives. He gives us space to dream.

But individual encouragement can be meaningless if we don't know what it is that drives us. When we've been shaped by the world, it can be so difficult to understand what our God-given passions actually are.

And so, before we can even come to the question of understanding our callings, we first have to understand our identities. We have to tackle the most ancient of all philosophical questions: *Who am I? What defines me? What is my identity?*

IDENTITY BEFORE DESTINY

Each of us has a history, a personal story that gives meaning to our lives—and also to our fears. Often those main storylines are colored not by strong and encouraging narratives but by anxious thoughts of uncertainty, bad experiences with home and family, traumatic events at school, and demoralizing words from our elders and peers.

Woven into my own life are childhood memories of the apartheid system in South Africa. I grew up in a rural area of the country firmly in the grip of those who believed in the separation of races. I never embraced those prejudices even though I attended, as required by law, an all-white school and eventually university. Like it or not—and I do not—the very system I loathed so much also provided the privileges of education denied to the vast majority of black people. In small ways I tried to stand against the system—leading our student union in protest against the government of the day—but I have always been troubled by the fact that I could have done more. There were many times when I was afraid to put the call of justice above my own interest, for fear that my own life and livelihood would be put in danger. And even now, many years later, I cannot but think of those occasions when the oppressed cried out for a response, but I simply did not have the courage to break the laws of segregation and face the draconian consequences of prison.

In 2014's Oscar-winning film *Birdman*, Michael Keaton plays a washed-out actor trying to start his life again after a series of failed roles. But his efforts are haunted by the voice of the "Birdman," the superhero role that made him famous in his youth. This voice in his head tells him a story about his life—a story of failure and missed chances. It taunts him with memories of what he was and could have been, but now isn't. The continuing question running through the film is simple: Will he listen to that voice of failure, or will he dare to believe that he can flourish again?

How often do we hear similar voices that taunt us about our past mistakes, our failures, our missed opportunities? It can be so tempting to listen to them, to allow them to define us.

But we are new creations in Christ: "The old has gone, the new is here!" (2 Corinthians 5:17). The old, negative history has been reformed; the story of our lives has been retold. Those discouraging, dominant thoughts *seem* to determine our futures, but God can, in his abundant grace and love, reshape them.

That God's love reaches out to us is a defining characteristic of our Christian lives. He calls to us from the depths of his love for us. We are powerless without the energy of his love, which has been poured into our hearts by the Spirit who has been given to us (Romans 5:5). The Holy Spirit is the source of our confidence in the world.

Ultimately I have a choice. Which narrative of my life do I believe? Is it the negative or the positive? It is easy to say the latter. But how do I deal with the former, which seems integral to my identity and, if unchecked, determines my response to my calling? I need to take responsibility for living this renewed life to the full as Christ promised. To do so, I see my story in the light of his journeying with me through every season. In this way, the apparently dominant negative theme becomes a subsidiary motif and loses its power to shape my decisions for the future.

There is a moment in Beethoven's Seventh Symphony when a dramatic battle takes place between two keys—F major and A major. This battle reflects the psychological struggle in Beethoven's own life. In the symphony, written after he had been deaf for many years, the F-major key represents the depression, frustration, and despair that he so often felt at being alienated from the world and from his own work. The despondency and downward spiral of depression start out as the dominant mode, but out of its depths, Beethoven introduced the A-major key, which represents life and love and beauty and hope. With the orchestra in full throttle, he determined to show the A-major theme of joy and love drowning out the F-major theme of despondency, thus establishing a sound of such boldness and confidence in life and the future as to be unforgettable. Even in the depths of his anguish, Beethoven chose to follow the positive, life-affirming narrative rather than slip into the resigned acceptance of his own weakness.

As my wife and I heard this symphony at the annual music festival in Verbier, Switzerland, set against the grandeur of the Swiss Alps, I realized again that, as Beethoven did, I have a choice: to follow the narrative that leads to life, or to succumb to the presenting turmoil that would rob me of my calling.

You may well have a distorted view of life or very low self-esteem. Perhaps you struggle to face the real you and want to live another's story. This is a huge danger; it is one of the great pressures put on you through social media. The temptation to post stories and images that enhance your personal standing is rife.

Recent polls showed that online users are creating false memories and identities, and they can no longer distinguish fact from fiction. The poll found that the fear of being boring and the envy of other people's lives caused two-thirds of users to lie about what they had been doing. One-fifth of those in their early twenties admitted that their online identities bore no resemblance to real life, and one in three personal posts were fabricated—a vacation that appeared so much more exciting than it was, a cool nightclub scene the poster didn't attend.[3]

It is so easy to create an avatar that represents a better self. And a growing number of young people admit that they feel shame about their untruths and cannot live up to their online images. So often what we imagine about ourselves crowds out the genuine voices that make us who we are.

True identity cannot be self-motivated; it is given by God. Our tasks are to live out our true callings as uniquely shaped by God.

I once sat down with a well-known Christian leader. I remember my shock when he told me that he really hated himself. Unsure of his own identity, he felt alienated and alone: a spirit trapped in a person he loathed. He had to pursue his calling in spite of persistent self-questioning. It was so difficult to know what to say. Outwardly, his life was successful and his ministry anointed. Inwardly, he was struggling.

John the Baptist attracted attention at the start of his ministry, and the leaders in Jerusalem sent priests and Levites to ask him "who he was" (John 1:19). He knew exactly who he was and who he was not, saying clearly, "I am not the Messiah" (v. 20).

He was pressed three times for his identity. He denied being Elijah the prophet. It was a kind of guessing game. So often when we meet people, we ask questions about their families, where they live, who they know. We try to find a box to put them in.

Finally John was asked, "What do you say about yourself?" (v. 22). John answered, "I baptize with water" and added that there was "one who comes after me, the straps of whose sandals I am not worthy to untie" (vv. 26–27).

We learn a good lesson, vital to understanding our calling, from this interchange: identity comes *before* destiny. We need to understand the person God created before we can begin to understand the person God created us to be.

Who I am, before *why* I am. So often we try to skip the first to end up with the second. We talk about our jobs in a functionally defining way, as if to say, *This is my destiny and my identity rolled into one.* But that is a mistake. I think of a friend whose identity was so tied up in his work as an accountant that he had a near breakdown when he left his job. After he left the office, he began the painful process of asking, "Who am I?"

We often talk about someone having an "identity crisis." In

reality, very few people go through life without facing real questions about their identities.

I know a young woman who held a senior position in an advertising firm but took time away from work to bring up her two small children. She struggled for years to rediscover her true identity, as her days were filled with mundane chores and she could no longer rely on her position at work to define her. And yet she knew that for that season of her life, her primary calling was to her family. She took on some part-time work to break the routine of the day and gradually grew to enjoy her decision to be at home. And then her calling changed as the circumstances changed. The children grew up and she could go back to full-time work. But she had learned a great lesson: she knew that she did not need to have her identity defined by her job. She was freer and happier in her own skin for being the person God wanted her to be. Through all the changes, God's love was the constant.

Then there was Sam, who had decided to leave the armed forces after serving for ten years. He experienced a long period of grave self-reflection, as his identity had been tied up in the military; he had to begin again to discover who he was in Christ. His discovery, too, was profound. He did not need to rely on his rank to know that he was valued by God.

The question is not only, "Who am I?" but, "Who am I *in Christ?*" I am defined in relationship with someone else. I am no longer the arbiter of success in my life. I am loved by someone else. The focus shifts to another person. In the words of Saint Paul, "For to me, to live is Christ and to die is gain" (Philippians 1:21). I am moving away from myself as the center and going toward Christ as the center. This is a hugely significant shift. This realization that life is best savored when lived for Christ is the key to living well. It moves the center of gravity from me to him, and, in that shift, is the very basis of finding my real calling.

Our destinies are what he calls us to, but they are never a

substitute for our identities—knowing who we are, knowing that we are uniquely and passionately loved by God. And for a good reason: in a fast-paced digital world, and in a world in which job changes are frequent, it is hard to find the constant thread that will keep us centered throughout our lives. If we come to the end of a phase at work, then we are tempted to think of ourselves as having no further value. But if we are secure in our identities, we know that the end of an era is not the end of our destinies. There is always more to come.

The world tells us that when we have become successful and have created names for ourselves, then we have identities. But with Christ this is flipped on its head. Our identities are secure through all the shifting sands of time. We are his beloved, his children. It is *from* that place of a secure identity that we can step into our callings, and not the other way around.

CHRIST-STYLE LIVING

You need to have a clear, God-shaped view of your true identity. No matter what others say about you—whether you are unemployed or employed, whether you have a history of failures behind you or a catalogue of success—you are infinitely worthy, chosen, valued. No matter whether you are a charity worker, a managing director of an investment bank, a teacher, or a postman, you are loved and have eternal significance. It is only once you grasp this that you can step into your calling, because it is only easy and natural to serve and live for others when you first know how loved you are: "We love because [God] first loved us" (1 John 4:19).

It is a simple truth that we cannot give what we haven't got. It is only once our love tanks have been so filled to overflowing by our heavenly Father that we can then give to others out of the overflow. This overflow of our hearts is manifest in Christ-style living.

Christ-style living is distinctive and should be instantly recognizable. It tries to make the most of every moment, emitting a "pleasing aroma" (2 Corinthians 2:15) in our workplaces, our relationships, our homes, our vacations, and even our sweaty gyms. Those who live this way do so because they know *why* they are living. They live for others, not themselves.

So my accountant friend who had the identity crisis when his job ended need not have feared, nor Sam when he left the army. Their identities were secure in Christ, who shifts our attitudes, activities, perspectives, and motivations away from ourselves and toward others, whom we regard as more important than ourselves. This is revolutionary in the workplace. Understanding that we are known by God as unique individuals created by him—loved by him—produces an antidote to the daily fear, anxiety, and corrosive inhumanity of living solely for personal gain. Being loved, known, and called by God is the trinity forming the basis of our confidence in the world.

This truth was illustrated to me vividly by a woman working behind a coffee kiosk at the airport in Austin, Texas. Her whole day consisted of serving coffee to harassed and time-constrained commuters. I was due to catch an early flight, and, feeling groggy and out of sorts, I went to buy a cup of coffee at the stand. The lady was cheerfulness itself at a time when I was anything but. She inquired how I took my coffee with what appeared to be a genuine interest. She detected through my accent that I was not from Texas, assuming that coffee was as strange a beverage to me as my accent was to her. "Tea," she announced, "does not do it for me." She asked me if I would like to try an additional flavoring, telling me that cinnamon was her favorite. She urged me to cheer up my day by ordering something different. All the while she was encouraging others in their orders.

Curiosity, or the cinnamon, got the better of me, and I asked why she seemed to take such an interest in her job. "Oh," she replied, with a smile that still pops up in my mind years later, "I want all my customers to have the best day possible. I try to give them a little piece of happiness to send them on their way. You know, I really love my job. I'm so grateful to have it. It gets me out of bed early. It's my tiny contribution to life."

Although this woman was up at the crack of dawn and on her feet all day, her orientation was outward, to others, away from herself. I scurried off, leaving her to spice up others' coffees along with their lives.

She had a simple job, but it was one that she was determined to use to its maximum. She saw beyond the mundane nature of her work to the difference she could make to others.

You need to start in the right place. If you view God as someone out to get you, to cramp your life and impede your pleasures, then you will see life in much the same way.

However, if you see him for who he is—an amazing, loving, gracious God who is out to find the best for you and is prepared to guide and help you through the tough times—then in Christ, your life will be full to overflowing. Your image of him, and his in you, projects and shapes your life.

You can only build an effective Christian life when you have a "settled core": an inner self "hidden with Christ" (Colossians 3:3). When you go to the gym or a Pilates class, your instructor might encourage you to build core strength, as it is vital for balance and keeping the body frame strong. So it is with the Christian life. You need to take the basics seriously and, from a secure identity, develop core relational strength. This is particularly important when you have to withstand the attacks of the enemy, whose sole task is to knock you off balance. To know your identity in Christ and to be strengthened in your basic relationship with him is a virtuous cycle of paramount importance to following your calling in the world.

God stretches our faith in order to prepare us to receive his promises. That often requires painful rewiring. We need updating, just as an old house may need rewiring. The old electrical wires might be out of date and dangerous, so change is necessary. No one likes going through this process of spiritual reorientation, but that is how we grow. I know of no one who has wanted to find a true identity in Christ and build a growing trust in the Lord who has not gone through a painful readjustment, perhaps many times, so motives, actions, ambitions, desires, and aspirations are radically pointed and repointed to Jesus. There must be radical abandonment of confidence in ourselves and an equally progressive growth in dependence on Christ.

So often, in the rough-and-tumble of the world, we drift away from intimacy with Christ. We act out of anger, resentment, or frustration. We assimilate too closely to the world. He needs to bring us back to our core identity in him so that we can hear his voice as he moves us on. Only when we have the comfort of our relationship with God can we confidently confront the callings that God has placed on our lives.

Orientating ourselves to hear God is the best thing we can do. We put ourselves in that place when we are obedient, open, and willing to learn. That is our part of preparing for his calling. It is proximity that matters. Our whole object of living is to take up his promise: "Draw near to [me], and [I] will draw near to you" (James 4:8 ESV). The rest is up to him. But we need to take those steps that lead us to stand under his grace, ready to receive his promises, his calling.

There is a penetrating question in Jeremiah 30:21: "Who is he who will devote himself to be close to me?"

I hope as you continue to read, you will answer, "I am."

—— TWO ——

CALLED TO ENGAGE

I HAVE SPENT THE APPRECIABLE PART OF ADULTHOOD LIVING in what appears to many to be two separate worlds. The first is the financial and business world, and the other is the church-based preaching and teaching world. You might assume that these worlds inevitably collide—after all, it can be so easy to disconnect our spiritual and religious lives from the wider working world of business and finance. The cutthroat world of commercial competition can be difficult to reconcile with the collective life of a Christian community. And yet Paul reminds us in his letter to the Colossians that "in [Christ] all things hold together" (Colossians 1:17).

I have come back to this verse again and again throughout my career, in humble recognition that there is only one Lord. The Lord of mercy is the Lord of the money markets. The Lord of prayer is the Lord of profit. The Lord of compassion is the Lord of competition. There really is only one sphere of influence: the kingdom of God. There Christ Jesus operates as Lord in our lives and in the world. Christ himself is the cornerstone and crossover point. By his Spirit he enables us to take the truths that are recorded for us in the Bible and translate them into day-to-day practical realities. He is our anchor as he aligns our wills to his. We must take hold of this truth in order to find our callings.

It is often said that we are *in* but not *of* the world. And while it is true that we are called to exemplify a different way of living, an

23

overemphasis on this idea can leave the impression that we have no real connection with secular society. Very often, wrong teaching has persuaded people that a kind of emigration from real life, in all its brokenness, is what is needed in order to live out a Christian calling. This idea results in an unrealistic gathering of like-minded (but angular) people who wish to remove themselves from reality, believing it to be a source of wickedness and not wishing to be tainted by association. Yet, in all the letters to the churches in the book of Revelation, God never called his people to leave their churches, even though those churches did some horrendous things. The call was to stay and to bring change. And the same is true when it comes to our engagement with the world. After all, we should never forget John 3:16: "For God so loved the world . . ."

This call to engagement can be difficult for a Christian. After all, this is a place that has decided to try to run its economies, societies, and structures without reference to the God who created and sustains it. We are called to do no less than our part, with God, to straighten what Immanuel Kant called the "crooked timber of humanity."[1] And we can only do so through the power of Jesus Christ.

There have been many occasions when I have felt the desire to leave the harsh competitiveness of the business world. It's tough; one feels the heat daily. And it seems so at odds with anything that could remotely be thought of as Christian. The nonprofit sector seems so attractive by comparison and, above all, appears to have an inherent purpose that I could only dream of.

I remember a time when one of these bouts was upon me. We were in the midst of a major transaction, advising one of the world's largest resource companies on its future strategy. It was harsh, the hours were long, and the client was demanding. I was tempted to throw in the towel and walk away from it all. I know we all have these moments when life just doesn't seem to make sense—and not only on Monday mornings. At times it is a passing thought:

Why am I doing this? At other times, it is the deep frustration of purposelessness. The grass of the nonprofit sector—or any other business—seems so much greener than the occasional tufts of green that mark the rough ground of the financial world.

In these times, I have formed a habit of turning to God to give me perspective on the frustration I am facing.

I cannot say I have ever heard the audible voice of God, but in the midst of this difficult time, I sensed a word of encouragement. And one phrase in particular made a great impression. There was weight to it, as if it were being cemented into me. A profound sense of calling, the very opposite of what I had been going though, lifted my spirit; and I had an overwhelming impression of Christ intervening in my life.

I sensed him saying, *"I am strengthening you in the world, for the world."*

In an instant I could see a purpose to what I had been going through. The grimness didn't just disappear, but somehow the knowledge that the unrelenting stress had a deeper value brought me out of that black hole. I learned a lesson then. The demands of the world are tough, but I developed a pattern of trying to coax myself through each of these attacks in the knowledge that God had called me to that place and would provide the strength that I would need for it.

I believe that this phrase was meant for me at that specific time, but it is also of much wider application to all of us who are at work in the world. Above all, it means accepting a full calling *in* the workplace to fulfill God-given plans *for* the workplace.

I don't have to tell you what it's like to work under the pressure of daily professional demands. The challenges of the competitive market economy take their toll on all of us. This is as true for an accountant as it is for a teacher facing exacting performance targets. No one is exempt. Deadlines need to be met and are set to maximize performance in a short time period. Relationships are strained, and temptations abound to cut corners or blame others or be a little greedy.

We must keep in mind that it is precisely *this world* that we are called to engage with. Jesus could not have been clearer in John 17 when he asked God not to take his disciples *out* of the world but to remain with them *in* the world: "My prayer is not that you take them out of the world but that you protect them from the evil one" (v. 15). It is Christ's desire for us to be made strong so that we remain in the world as salt and light (Matthew 5:13–16). His instrument for strengthening us is Scripture (John 17:14, 17).

STRENGTHEN THE CORE

The instrument by which Christ strengthens us is the Holy Spirit. As Paul wrote to the Ephesians: "I pray that out of his glorious riches he may strengthen you with power through his spirit in your inner being" (Ephesians 3:16). It is the Spirit who comes alongside *us* to increase the tenacity of our weak human frames. He is the one who motivates us to live each day for Christ, working where we have been called with vigor and passion.

Our calling to engage with the world can be felt in all areas of our lives—our family lives, our social lives, our leisure time. But one of the most important areas where we are likely to feel the gentle (and sometimes not-so-gentle) pull of the Spirit is in our work lives.

And yet the idea that God might call us into the humdrum and daily grind of the workplace is a fairly novel one to many people. There's often a perception among Christians that our callings should have a distinctly religious flavor. Being called to full-time pastoral ministry, or evangelism, or missionary work with a charity—that fits with what people expect. But when I say that I felt called to investment banking, people often raise an eyebrow or two!

The NBA superstar LeBron James once posted on social media, "I was born with a God given talent, but I PROMISE you when the bright lights go down I am grinding it out and working my tail off to get better."[2] God doesn't just call us into the bright lights and moments of euphoria. He calls us to the daily toil of the workplace as well.

This view that God and grind don't mix has led to many Christians suffering inferiority complexes regarding their vocations. I remember talking to one young student who dreamed of becoming a lawyer, but all around him his Christian friends were thinking about full-time Christian work. Despite his dreams, he couldn't help but feel that he was letting God down by not doing the same.

How sad it is that someone with such a God-given passion would feel guilty about following it!

As we pursue our callings, what matters is that we make Jesus' name known in the world, that we live in light of the great story of God's love and the great hope of the Christian faith. Larry Page, the CEO of Google's parent company Alphabet, Inc., once observed that most of the big companies that fail do so because they "missed the future"—they did not see where the world was going.[3] While Christians might not know what is right around the corner, we *do* know where the world is going. We know that at the end of all things, God will make all things new. We know that Christ's death has overcome the darkness, and through his life-giving resurrection we wait patiently for his return.

The world tries to atomize society, but we are called to draw together the spiritual, ethical, and vocational aspects of life. Above all, we are to live as if these aspects of life were in fact one. In this way we become motivated and strengthened, not only to pursue our individual callings but to reach out to the hurting world around us; not only to pursue justice but to bring reconciliation to a divided world.

But we cannot be strengthened in a vacuum. A couple of hours a week in church may focus attention and even reorder priorities, but it is in the daily life of the workplace where we need to "practice the presence of God." We all need to take time out to rest and respect Sunday. But the workplace should be a continuation of our worship and love of God, not an interruption of God's work from Sunday to Sunday. In perhaps the most famous verse in John's gospel, we read that "God so loved the world that he gave his one and only Son, that whoever believes in him shall not perish but have eternal life" (John 3:16). But I often wish the next verse were as famous: "For God did not send his Son into the world to condemn the world, but to save the world through him" (v. 17).

Often we need reminders that work is good. It is an activity in which we can experience joy. It is not just a grim grind, a necessary evil, or a heavy-hearted means to pay the bills. From the beginning of Genesis, we learn that work is service. It is for the common good, and it retains this intrinsic value, albeit tarnished. God is interested in our work, he loves us for sticking at it, and he rewards us (although not necessarily financially) when it is done well. Work is the place chosen by Christ himself where we spend the majority of our time on earth.

Yet I have spoken to many people whose energy levels and desires to achieve a fixed purpose are frequently at odds with the often-boring nature of what the workplace offers. Quite a lot of work is humdrum, administrative, and tedious. How do we cope?

Michael works as a manager on a farming estate. He loves the countryside but struggles with the day-to-day repetitive nature of his work. "It's not my dream job, Ken," he told me, "but does that mean it's not right for me?"

My advice is simple: strengthen the core and the chores will become bearable. At the core of each of us is an identity secure in Christ, which leads to an ongoing, unbroken relationship with him. Out of that relationship we are convicted, not once but daily, that we have the talent to fulfill our God-given callings. This is why and how we do what we do. Relationship is what holds us together.

Some people wake up each day knowing that there is nothing else they would rather do than go to work. They absolutely love their jobs. I knew an architect who used to get increasingly excited as the weekend progressed, until he was almost on a high on Sunday evenings knowing he would be back in the office on Monday morning.

Others are more ambivalent; sometimes we're in a good season and sometimes not. This is when we need to remind ourselves that we enjoy the essence of what we are doing but struggle with the menial tasks, the prevalent bureaucracy, the high stress levels, and the stagnant downtime. Again, it is the clarity of our callings that carries us through the chores.

One of the great fallacies we face is that every day should be a peak of fulfilled activity. The world seldom works that way. It's an unreal and unsustainable view. So we need to develop an understanding of the rhythm of our work and begin to let God, through his Spirit, enable us to work well even when there appears to be little action around and the days lengthen with frustrating chores. Perseverance is part of life!

I once heard a story of a famous rock star who was struggling to adjust to the dull monotony of normal life, as he was so used to the adrenaline rush of the stage. He went through every day expecting to experience the moments of euphoria that he felt when performing to thousands at a concert, and he found himself feeling empty and unfulfilled when those moments didn't appear. So he went to see his counselor, expecting some clear, quick, and helpful advice. To his annoyance, the counselor simply said, "When you wake up each morning, make your own bed, polish your shoes [this was some time ago!], and make your own cup of tea. Come back and let me know how you get on."

Despite his skepticism, the rock star came back the next week having learned a great lesson. The little acts of normality had helped him see that all of us have to get through chores and can't expect every second of the day to be pumped. Depression and low feelings are often fueled by unrealistic expectations. We need to take owner-ship of and embrace the little acts that make up such a huge part of our lives. If we are constantly searching for the next euphoric expe-rience, we'll enter into a dangerous cycle.

Not only are we to be strengthened at the workplace for our own sake, but also our purpose is "for" the world. I love the line in the Lord's Prayer: "your will be done, on earth as it is in heaven" (Matthew 6:10). As translated, the order is hugely significant. Earth comes first. Unlike most other religions, Christianity encourages us to be agents of change and, through the power of God, to restore this world to wholeness.

MAKE AN IMPRINT

The Nelson Mandela Foundation once ran a campaign asking people to make an imprint. Mandela himself, and other charities and initiatives, proposed making his birthday an annual celebration of his ideals and vision. He hoped that "Mandela Day," which he described as "not . . . a holiday, but a day devoted to service," would be a global call to action to show that each individual has the power to influence the world.[4] The image for the campaign was an impression of Mandela's hand on a beach. One could see clearly the displacement of the sand and the appearance of the hand and the fingers. That is what an imprint does; it leaves a mark. It shifts other things out of the way.

Imprinting the Spirit of God in our lives is critical. And as we are imprinted, so we are called to imprint the world. Like the hand-print on the beach, we are called to imprint the Spirit of God onto the world. This imprint is the love of Christ, which allows for the flourishing of humanity. There can be no greater impact than lives that demonstrate such an imprint, such a stamp of love on our com-munities and commercial activities.

We learn a great deal about making an imprint from Caleb in

the Old Testament. He was an extraordinary man. Five times it is said that Caleb "served the LORD wholeheartedly" and that he had a "different spirit."

In Numbers 13–14, we read that twelve people, including Caleb, were called to go on a journey to discover what the land of Canaan was like. This was no different from many of our tasks today. Consultants are asked to undertake "scoping exercises" or feasibility studies for complex business projects, or to conduct risk analyses to determine whether a project is financially viable. And anyone who has been to one of these "report back" meetings, PowerPoint at the ready, understands the opposition faced by Caleb and Joshua.

Twelve men visited the same site, met the same people, learned the same facts, saw the same topography, and heard the same reports. On their return, ten of them said, effectively, "You must be joking. We can't go there. The people are giants. The cities are fortified. We'll never make it." ("The costs will overrun, the terrain is impossible, the technical feasibility is negative," and so on.)

Yet Caleb, who followed the Lord wholeheartedly, agreed with Joshua and said, "The land we passed through and explored is exceedingly good. If the LORD is pleased with us, he will lead us into that land, a land flowing with milk and honey, and will give it to us. . . . The LORD is with us. Do not be afraid" (Numbers 14:7–9). Caleb trusted God. He saw the world through the lens of God's character.

There is a story of two executives who visited Indonesia to test the market for shoe sales. One reported back that few of the inhabitants wore shoes and concluded that there was no point in setting up a factory. The other executive looked at the same situation but saw the opportunity of selling shoes to the millions of shoeless Indonesians. Same place, same facts, different perspective.

I believe that our world—with all its tortuous opportunities to live independently of the original prospectus, the Bible—is a world that is "exceedingly good" because Jesus came to conquer all those forces that corrupt and to make a way for creation to become as God intended. He can make boredom bearable and toil tolerable for those who see through the lens of his work. He also makes joy incomparable, far greater than any other experience of it in the world.

If only we could see the world differently, as Caleb did. If we see it as the other spies did, we see giants who are too difficult to defeat. We are negative, complaining, untrusting, and unable to advance. However, if we believe and trust in a powerful God, then we see that the world is "exceedingly good" and that, through the power of God, we can move toward our God-given callings and not be afraid. We see milk and honey flowing from the goodness of people whose lives are changed.

But how exactly do we make an imprint? How can we be of any use to God in the workplace?

TAKING GOD'S PERSPECTIVE

I was talking to a friend a few months ago who was trying to understand what it means to be a Christian witness in the secular workplace. What does it look like when someone enters the workplace with a uniquely Christian calling?

"Imagine someone working in a junior role for a big accounting firm," he said to me, "who talks to her colleagues about Jesus whenever the opportunity arises and invites them along to church, but never really gets anywhere with it. After putting up with it for a while, her colleagues get bored; they shut her down whenever she tries to turn the conversation to matters of faith. They don't give her a chance to witness. How can she have a calling in the workplace in that situation? How can she be a witness to Jesus when nobody wants to hear it?"

This is an all-too-common situation. Christians are going into their places of work desperate to make Jesus known, but they are repeatedly confronted by coworkers who just don't want to know.

But my friend's response to this situation also left me feeling downcast. He couldn't envisage a Christian calling in the workplace that went beyond straight-up evangelism. If the words of the gospel were falling on deaf ears, he thought, then what more could a Christian do?

This mind-set is a problem in many parts of the church. This narrow, reductionist perspective about what it means to have a calling is hamstringing the Christian witness in the workplace. It alienates and divorces Christianity from the world.

Jesus told us in Matthew's gospel that we, as Christians, are called to be salt to the earth and light to the world (Matthew 5:13–16). Part of our common Christian calling is that we transform *this* life. We are not called simply to win converts with words, to drag people onto the lifeboat of faith as if saving them from the stricken *Titanic*. Christianity is not a faith for isolationists. The gospel is ultimately about this world being redeemed by trusting Jesus. Evangelism is certainly a key part of the gospel message—and it may well be a key part of our callings—but it has a twin called *transformation*. Both are integral to God's reconciliation of humanity.

We are called into the workplace to transform the workplace. To bring a little slice of God's divine, transforming goodness. To be salt and light in the way we work. But still this question remains: *How* do we make an imprint? *How* can we be salt and light? *How* can we carry out God-given callings in the workplace?

The simple answer is that we are called to act with love in everything we do. In Matthew's gospel, Jesus gave us two commandments. The first is quoted straight from Deuteronomy: "Love the Lord your God with all your heart and with all your soul and with all your mind" (Matthew 22:37). And the second, he said, is like it: "Love your neighbor as yourself" (v. 39). This is the general calling all Christians receive—to love our neighbors and to love our God.

Who are our neighbors? In the workplace, it is anyone with whom we engage: shareholders, clients or customers, colleagues, suppliers, and the local communities in which our businesses or charities operate on a day-to-day basis. It is the "invisible partners" on whom we depend, and who depend on us in turn, but are rarely acknowledged in the quarterly review. We, as Christians, are called to love them not with an agenda or an ulterior motive, but simply for the sake of it. We are called to act with fairness, honesty, and integrity in places of work that can often be places of deceit, cutthroat competition, and selfish ambition. We are called to glorify God in our daily interactions and to live lives marked by worship of God and love of our neighbors.

Trying to live such lives in the workplace can sometimes feel like fruitless endeavors. It can be deeply disheartening to see attempts at love, honesty, and integrity fall on hard and unresponsive soil. Earlier in my career, not long after I had taken a more senior role in the firm where I was working, I pushed for the firm to start investing more in employees' mental health. I wanted to see our company providing counseling services and taking a more proactive approach to relieving work-based stress. Now, of course, such services are becoming popular as employers wake up to the dangers of burnout and stress-related conditions, but at the time many of my suggestions went completely unheeded. The old model of employment tended to see employees as a commodity from which to extract the maximum short-term profit, and there was little appetite for investing in long-term employee health, especially when it came to the misunderstood issues of mental welfare.

At such times it is important to remember that while the world might judge by outcomes and results, God does not. So we shouldn't judge the success of our actions by the standards of the world. There is value in the act of love itself. There was value simply in the fact that I was pushing for a change, even if my arguments were not successful. In our hospitals and our prisons, Christians have always been found loving the broken and the dying, the criminal and the drug addicted. We might hope for change, but we don't commit to loving such people on the basis that change will arise. We love them because they are children of God, worthy of love just as they are, in all their brokenness.

God calls us to use our God-given skills and talents in unique ways to further his kingdom. Just as God called Moses, Gideon, and Joseph in their places of work, so God calls all of us into specific places at specific times, to transform places of darkness into places of light.

One of the greatest problems facing Christianity today is a refusal to believe that God could possibly care about our individual futures, that God could care about our day-to-day lives or have plans for us outside of a particularly religious call. We're often fine with the idea that he might call other people, but there can be a deep insecurity about whether God could possibly use us. When it comes to *my* calling and *my* future, we fear that God has forgotten us.

Of course, it's relatively easy to understand Christian calling when it relates to those who fulfill some specifically Christian responsibility in their places of work. Pastors, worship leaders, and high-profile evangelists can make a clear link between their work and their God-given callings. So, too, can those who inhabit positions of power and prestige, or those whose work has an obvious positive impact on society. They might still doubt it, but we can easily imagine that politicians, teachers, charity workers, and doctors find it easier to rest assured that their work is an embodiment of their Christian calling.

But what about those who are not going to cure cancer, deliver aid, or evangelize from a platform? How can they see a calling that is unique to them?

Part of the answer lies in trying to view our work through the eyes of God, rather than through the eyes of the world. The world is utilitarian in its judgments and standards. The more obvious good we do and the more people we positively impact, the more the world will judge our efforts worthwhile. But this is not God's perspective.

Mark's gospel describes an occasion when Jesus was in the temple courtyard, watching the crowds put money into the treasury. Some very wealthy people poured huge sums of money into the collection plate, probably with lots of trumpeting and self-promotion. And then in slipped a poor widow, who put into the collection two small copper coins—barely enough to buy a meal of grain.

The donations of the rich would go on to do great works through the temple. They'd feed the priests, clothe the poor, buy new ornaments to adorn the spaces of worship. Compared to that, the widow's offering was practically worthless in the eyes of the world. But it was not worthless to Jesus.

> Calling his disciples to him, Jesus said, "Truly I tell you, this poor widow has put more into the treasury than all the others. They all gave out of their wealth; but she, out of her poverty, put in everything—all she had to live on." (Mark 12:43–44)

In the end, even the greatest of our works will be forgotten by the world. All our efforts will be dust and ashes in the face of God's eternal glory. There is a beautiful simplicity to that verse in Isaiah 40: "The grass withers and the flowers fall, but the word of our God endures forever" (v. 8). When it comes to the worthiness of our callings, we need to take a divine perspective and remember that God's standards are not like those of the world.

Some people are called to do great works—govern countries, direct relief efforts, evangelize millions. And some people are called to do small acts of service—pour coffee with a smile, sweep the streets, bake a cake for their neighbors. But God does not look at these things and see them as inconsequential. To him they are beautiful outpourings of his spirit.

A calling to serve God in the workplace might be to revive a failing company. Or perhaps it is to be a loyal and faithful friend to a coworker going through a tough time. Though the world may judge one as more significant than the other, God does not.

FOMO

Insecurity about the legitimacy of one's calling is not the only great obstacle facing those currently entering the workplace. Many adults in their twenties currently inhabit a state of deferred adolescence. Whereas graduating from college or celebrating a twenty-first birthday once marked the end of this stage of life, adulthood is postponed for some as the job market shrinks and the perennial question "What am I going to do with my life?" becomes paralyzing. Commitment is therefore deferred across the board: what job to take, where to live, and whether or not to be in a relationship. There is a new subgeneration of "gradolescents" developing; that is, graduates who have not yet fully emerged to face the sharp winds of the working world.

Above all, there is a huge increase in the choices available to younger men and women that were not available to the previous generations. More choices do not guarantee an easier life; often they are paralyzing rather than liberating. Overwhelmed by possibilities, these young people are gripped by FOMO: Fear Of Missing Out. This fear is crippling many people who believe they are stuck and worry that making one choice excludes the benefits of another.

Martin is a young consultant strategist. He is bright, well educated, and perfectly capable of achieving a huge amount for the kingdom of God, to which he is devoted. He completed college—not at the top of his class, but high enough. He had many job opportunities even in this harsh environment. He started working for a charity and then took time out to travel. He entered into a relationship but without any real commitment to it long-term. We met to talk about his future. On the face of it, he had options others only dream of, and yet at his core he was unfulfilled. As we talked, it became clear that he was beset by an overriding fear of missing out on the many opportunities that could be available to him in the future. Accepting a job meant excluding another that might turn up later. To be too intentional about one woman excluded the possibility of meeting someone else later who was more perfect. To commit to sharing a flat with two good friends ended the possibility of finding a better place closer to the center of London. Church life was a matter of observation without involvement—watching but not willing to engage too deeply. He felt that he was strapped to the starting blocks, ready to move forward but unable to start the race.

Many have similar stories. I've noticed a pervasive, chronic expectation among young adults that there exists a perfect life path where every variable is lined up: financial resources, future prospects, relationships, and so on. On that path, choices would practically make themselves.

Martin could not see the tape at the end of the race and spent needless time debating why he was on the starting block. I understood his angst. We talked at length about how to fight and not fuel his FOMO. He needed to realize that *in Christ, you don't miss out.* The principal problem is *who* determines the missing out. If it is the individual, then *choice is the enemy of commitment.* But if we believe that the future belongs to God and he is able to lead us through the fear trap, then a new perspective takes hold. Fear diminishes as favor increases. It starts with a simple step. Once we have faith that only God holds our futures, we accept the wonderful truth that those who put their trust in him will have no reason to fear missing out in life.

Unchecked, FOMO can grow into a hunger for accumulating possessions as well as experiences. This is the problem behind another popular acronym: YOLO (You Only Live Once).

I think of a friend who was buying a fancy new car. "Why not?"

he said. "You can't take it with you." I know that mantra well. I have heard it said many times by the rich and powerful, but also by those of lesser means as a prelude to some extravagance. Why not enjoy life—buy a new toy, go on vacation, have an affair, tick the so-called bucket list of the hundred things you must do before you die? After all, whatever James Bond might say, you only live once. Not twice.

In a physical sense, it is, of course, true that "you can't take it with you." We will all die physically. But that is not the end of the story. The promise of Jesus, underwritten by his unique resurrection from the dead, is that new life is possible beyond death. We leave behind our homes, our bank accounts, and all our physical assets, perhaps to be squabbled over. Even our marriages and relationships with our friends cease. But existence does not.

That's what's so incredible about the good news: for those who put their trust in Jesus, there is the promise of resurrection and eternal life! This life that Jesus calls us to will continue beyond physical death—and we *can* take it with us. Life in all its fullness starts now, at work, in our friendships, and in our communities. And it is forever.

My wife and I had John 10:10 printed on the front of our order of service at our wedding: "I have come that they may have life, and have it to the full." This verse is the foundation of our marriage and the single promise we have held on to most tightly throughout our life together. Against the prevailing belief in the world of a narrow-minded, miserly God, we need to live the truth that he is committed to abundance and to our flourishing in this life.

ETHOS AND THEOS

YOLO is either an invitation to binge in indulgence or an expression of the desire to make every moment pleasing to God. When Paul wrote to the Colossians, he admonished them to seize every opportunity to work for the Lord, enjoying all the good things that God had given, and to share those with others: "Whatever you do, work at it with all your heart, as working for the Lord, not for human masters" (Colossians 3:23). This is the ethos at the heart of the Christian faith, although it can be difficult to identify within our wider society.

Ethos is the ingredient that establishes the dominant culture in an organization or a society. Ethos sets the way we behave and our reasons for doing so. Often we say that a company is a good place to work because it has a good culture—a good ethos.

Year after year in the United Kingdom, the John Lewis Partnership heads the list of the best companies to work for. It owns some of the largest department stores in the country, but crucially, it is *owned by* the employees, who divide the profits at the end of the year. John Lewis has established an incredibly positive central ethos to the company, helping it thrive.

And, of course, there are many examples of companies whose corrupt or negative ethos produce damaging results, both among the employees and in their performances. One of the most motivating tasks for those who are "in the world, for the world" is to bring about a whole-scale ethos change. In redirecting the objectives of commerce away from self-gratification and toward service to others, we serve God.

If we are filled with God's love, compassion, gentleness, and truth, then we have the power to transform the atmosphere around us. Conversely, if we are filled with bitterness, anger, jealousy, and hatred—even though we have smiles on our faces—the negativity can leak out and pollute our environments.

A teacher named Emily used to work alongside a bitter, unhappy colleague in the school where she taught. This colleague badmouthed parents and children, and she spoke with vitriolic passion about most things. Emily found it an impossible place to work. She shared her concern with her church small group, who encouraged her to worship, pray, and get right with God, so that when she walked into the staff room, the light of Jesus could shine there.

When she started to do this, she discovered something remarkable. As she prayed for this difficult colleague over a number of weeks, she was filled with love for her. The colleague was still bitter and foul-tempered, but Emily was able to see beyond the bitterness and respond in love. She began to see not a nasty and spiteful person but a broken and hurting child of God. She allowed the change within her to be revealed in her attitude. Each day Emily was able to walk into the staff room shining the love and grace of Christ. She said the difference her actions made was tangible; it was as if this colleague were struck dumb.

Once we are transformed into abundant living, it is impossible not to shine.

We are called to reflect a new humanity in our work. Our model is Christ, who came to perfect us. He worked not to make us more religious but more human. In the baptism narrative, when we read of the Holy Spirit coming on Jesus as a dove, we witness a moment of deep affirmation of his humanity, not of his divinity. If God had come down to imbue a man with divine propensities, we would expect him immediately to get to work on a series of miracles and other demonstrations of God's power. But he didn't. Instead Jesus was led into the desert to be tempted, a quintessentially human activity.

From the start of his ministry to the end, Jesus brought together the fallen parts of humanity by becoming one of us, experiencing the same stresses and strains of a broken world, and yet never letting the pressure lead him into sin. So we behave at work as carriers of this new humanity in a broken and dehumanized workplace. We are called to worship God in every area of our lives, including in our workplaces—to make our workstations our worship stations. We change the ethos by making the working environment more human and more attentive to people's needs, by establishing appropriate time for rest, and by ensuring that demands are reasonable and reporting lines are clear. That is how we fulfill Christ's calling, wherever and at whatever level we work.

I think it's worth noting that people work for a variety of reasons. For many, the primary purpose of their work is cash. Their principal motivation at work is the paycheck that funds their daily needs as well as their off-line pastimes, hobbies, and interests. They don't really want their jobs interfering with their lives. Their work is a means to an end—for example, to fund a new racing bike, an art collection, or an outdoor activity. Or simply to survive.

Others are motivated at work by their ambitions for a career. They desire to move up the career ladder, to expand their experiences, and to become more skilled in a particular area. Again, their work becomes subservient to satisfying their own desires and needs and is motivated primarily by the status and prestige that comes with promotion and expertise. I remember so well the tension at the time of annual performance reviews. Wanting to move ahead is a powerful drive.

Still others work for a cause. These people throw themselves into something much bigger than themselves, believing in the wider purpose of their work. Their desire is to make a difference in the world—to leave a mark in some way.

All of these are legitimate motivations. It is vital that we earn money in order to provide for our families and those we love. It is good that we take pride in our work and seek to push ourselves on to new challenges. It is certainly good to contribute to the world around us. However, too great a focus on cash, career, or cause can harbor dangers. So often I have noticed career-minded people become neurotic as they constantly try to gauge how they are shaping up to the expectations of their colleagues. If not checked, too great a focus on cash and earnings can rapidly lead to a disengaged interest toward both our work and our colleagues. The great danger of working for a cause, however noble, is that we can come to see our work in purely utilitarian terms. Rather than valuing the little things, we fixate on the bigger picture, the biggest social change.

Missing from all three of these is any sense of the value of work itself. We focus on greater and greater output—more cash, a greater career, a bigger cause—and neglect what we are putting in. In doing so, we tend to miss the opportunities that the workplace itself presents to us.

What we need is a calling. Those who see their work as a calling experience a rich integration in their lives. They sense a purpose, a direction to their activities. Work has intrinsic meaning, rather than being simply a means to an end. They feel that their whole personalities are flowing in and through their work. In many ways this is precisely what the Spirit of God does in our lives. When we are flowing with the Spirit, we are cooperating fully in our God-given callings. We are operating in that grace-zone where everything we do seems to come naturally. Far from being detached or self-centered, those who are "going with the flow" of their callings are highly motivated to enjoy what they are doing for its own sake. They love their work, can manage inevitable tensions that arise, and are welcomed by their colleagues, who sense something beyond the usual cash or career objectives.

As I have searched for my own grace-zone over the years, I have been constantly reminded of the words of Paul: "From one man he made all the nations, that they should inhabit the whole earth; and he marked out their appointed times in history and the boundaries of their lands" (Acts 17:26). God is not just interested in nations, of course. For individuals, too, he has marked out the times and the territories of our lives. Sometimes our callings will be a daily grind. But there will also be times of rich reward—periods of our lives when we are living in that grace-zone, feeling the Spirit of God flow through us and into the world.

Full living comes when we walk in lockstep with the Spirit. He reaches through us to the chaotic lives of our colleagues and friends. Because we receive life from Jesus, we can now give life. This is the transforming calling for all of us: to be changed by the Spirit and then be the change to those around us.

This "abundant" life speaks plainly, not some religious babble; drinks joyfully but not excessively; finds positive things to say about individuals; seeks to work better and go the extra mile in helping others flourish and fulfill their potentials. We're not called to be a tame sect of killjoys with a series of dos and don'ts (generally more don'ts than dos). Our call is the opposite: to live lives touched by the overwhelming joy of the Spirit, even in times of acute difficulty. Encouragement is a gift not meant exclusively for the Christian subculture. We are all called to speak words of encouragement to everyone. It's amazing how thoughtfully building up coworkers will transform our places of work.

The distinguished Catholic theologian Hans Küng described our mission in the world as one that would see "creation healed."[5] That is what Jesus came to do. That is our calling.

I am so often struck by the words, "Wake up, sleeper, rise from the dead, and Christ will shine on you" (Ephesians 5:14). It feels like a proverbial slap of my face to open my eyes to what God can do. I sense him saying, "I will awaken those who are asleep." Let us not slumber through our lives and miss out on what God can and will do through us.

When I sit at my desk in my study, I sit between a large mirror and the window. If I look to my left, I see myself, reflected back. If I look to my right, I see the world outside. But if I stand up and look in the mirror, I see myself *in the context of the wider world*.

This is our challenge today: to see our callings in the context of the wider world. We are not called to sit apart from the world, but to engage with it in the light of Christ; to see a wholeness seeping through every aspect of society. If, together, we rise to an openness to be stirred by the Spirit and to live out of the knowledge that nothing can unsettle the future if it is built on the values of Christ, then a new hope grips us and, like a virus, will infect the world around us. This is a supreme work of the Spirit of God. But he stirs only where he sees servants ready to work at healing a broken society.

Schubert's Symphony no. 8 is known as the "Unfinished Symphony," because it is missing the final movement. It stops, wherever it is played, after only the first two. The composer did not intend it to be left unfinished (and musicologists are divided over the reasons why he did not see it through), but no one could step into his shoes in order to make it complete. In many ways Jesus, too, left behind something that was unfinished. He left it to *us* to complete the work of establishing a community of love in the world. Our engagement with the world is how the world will come to know him.

Are we, like Caleb, willing to put our trust in God? To see the world God loves through his eyes, and genuinely believe that we have all that is necessary to live lives of such authenticity in the workplace as to draw our friends inevitably closer to Jesus?

——— THREE ———

CALLED TO FLOURISH

JOEY PRUSAK WAS AN EMPLOYEE AT THE ICE CREAM CHAIN Dairy Queen. One day, as he was serving customers their food, he noticed that a blind man had dropped a twenty-dollar bill on the floor. A lady standing in line quietly bent down and put the twenty dollars into her own pocket. Young Joey Prusak approached the lady, asking her to give the twenty-dollar bill back to the blind man. She refused, quite aggressively, claiming it was her own.

And then Joey did something very generous. Quietly, he opened up his own wallet and handed the blind man a twenty-dollar bill of his own. The man took the money gratefully, and the Dairy Queen resumed normal business.

A customer in line observed the whole episode and sent an e-mail to the Dairy Queen management, informing them of Joey's act of generosity. The DQ management then posted about it on Facebook, and the event went viral. A couple of days later, Joey received a call from the billionaire Warren Buffet, a big investor in Dairy Queen. He thanked Joey for showing such integrity and asked him to come to the next Dairy Queen investors' meeting. As Joey was an employee and representative of Dairy Queen, Buffet wanted him to be there as an integral part of the fabric of the organization.[1]

Joey's act of generosity inspired thousands of people to believe that they, too, could do something small to impact the world for good. It was a small act—with a huge impact.

And so it is with God. He takes our small acts of obedience or kindness or goodness and multiplies them for his good, and ours. So don't wait until you can do big things; start small.

Sometimes small seeds grow into large trees, and sometimes they fail to thrive. More often than not, small business ventures fail. But in the kingdom of God, small acts *always* have significant effects, though we may not always see them. God sees the attitude behind our actions, and he multiplies the results.

A tiny amount of yeast is put into the ingredients for making bread, and yet it enables the bread to grow several times its original size. God takes what we have, however small, and makes it significant.

You may relate to one or two of these:

+ "One day when I've got a decent house, *then* I'll be able to show hospitality."
+ "I haven't got enough money to give, but when I earn more I'll be really generous."
+ "In the future I'm going to talk to people about Jesus, but right now I don't feel confident."
+ "I have no sense of calling to *anything* specific in life."

Very often we wonder whether we have any gifts at all that can be used for the common good. It is easy to think we have nothing to offer.

A new junior colleague of mine lived with some others in a rented flat. There was nothing wrong with the flat except perhaps it was a little small and rather bare. But the fact that it wasn't his and wasn't particularly fancy made him think that the place wasn't nice enough to welcome anyone. As a result, he never wanted friends to meet there. He did not take into account that people would like to spend time with him, however small or bare or simple the place was.

God is interested in our lives right now, however bare or unimpressive or simple they may seem to us. He's interested in who we are and what we have, not what we do not have.

THE PROPHET'S WIDOW

We can learn a good deal about how little becomes large from the story of the prophet's widow, found in 2 Kings 4. It is a passage that I return to again and again, particularly when it looks like luck is running out. I know that *luck* is not the right word to use, but I feel it nonetheless when I get to the end of my trust-rope and wonder whether God will honor my small acts of obedience.

> The wife of a man from the company of the prophets cried out to Elisha, "Your servant my husband is dead, and you know that he revered the LORD. But now his creditor is coming to take my two boys as his slaves."
>
> Elisha replied to her, "How can I help you? Tell me, what do you have in your house?"
>
> "Your servant has nothing there at all," she said, "except a small jar of olive oil."
>
> Elisha said, "Go around and ask all your neighbors for empty jars. Don't ask for just a few. Then go inside and shut the door behind you and your sons. Pour oil into all the jars, and as each is filled, put it to one side."
>
> She left him and shut the door behind her and her sons. They brought the jars to her and she kept pouring. When all the jars were full, she said to her son, "Bring me another one."
>
> But he replied, "There is not a jar left." Then the oil stopped flowing.
>
> She went out and told the man of God, and he said, "Go, sell the oil and pay your debts. You and your sons can live on what is left." (vv. 1–7)

This story is about debt. Debt is brutal. Today people aren't claimed by their creditors as slaves for failure to pay an outstanding debt. We don't have—except in the appalling case of human trafficking—families sold into bondage. Still, debt is crippling, as anyone who has been in debt knows all too well. There is no escaping or wishing it away.

The prophet in the story revered God and was respected by others. But he got into such debt that his sons were on the verge of being sold. His destitute wife is not named—she is the everyperson of history who has been in a situation of facing problems beyond one's control. The debt was devastating, and there was no social security system. It is worth remembering, when we look at our personal debt and a debt-stricken world, that debt is a destroyer of hope.

The prophet's wife faced up to the facts of her situation and cried out to God. When she told the prophet Elisha what had happened, he asked her an utterly absurd question: "Tell me, what do you have in your house?" (v. 2). She replied that she had nothing. All her possessions would have been taken by the creditors and pawned. Bankruptcy had left her home practically bare.

She was trapped in the mind-set of despair, rejection, and poverty, and Elisha needed to change it. He asked her again, "What do you have?"

This time she said, "Your servant has nothing . . . except a small jar of olive oil" (v. 2).

"Nothing *except* . . ." The great encounter began as soon as she was *prepared to live by an exception*. Every worldview changes when we realize that the facts we seem to be facing and that seem so compelling are not the reality we live in.

For the first time, she became open to the possibility that she might have something, rather than being painfully aware of all she did not have. It is the possibility of God—an intervening God— that matters in these moments, and he wants us to look around and be prepared to use whatever we have in order to fulfill our callings. We often become so blinded by desperation that we cannot see what we already hold in our hands that might be used to further our callings. I hope the junior colleague I talked with understood what God can do, even with a small, sparsely furnished, rented flat.

Elisha instructed the prophet's widow, "Go around and ask all your neighbors for empty jars. Don't ask for just a few" (v. 3). Elisha's suggestion of not "just a few" was not an afterthought but an essential part of the miracle. Abundance was coming.

I have puzzled over why Elisha allowed this encounter with the widow to happen so publicly. This woman was already humiliated. She was alone and destitute. And it is more than likely that the neighbors were all aware of her plight. Why is it that Elisha wanted to involve them? Could it be that when God works a great miracle, he doesn't want simply a private transaction between the individual and God? Could it be that he wants the whole community to be involved? The miracle then becomes a witness to the community of God's provision, particularly for the most despairing.

The woman was obedient. She withdrew to her home and closed her door to the outside world with its judging eyes. She was alone with God and her family—without muttering that if her husband, a prophet no less, had not been so profligate, she would have been cared for. She began to pour from the little jar of olive oil. She poured and poured, and the oil in the jar increased as God met her needs. She had an encounter with God in her home with her sons around her. Every single jar was filled.

She had been in desperate need, and now she was revitalized. She had been discouraged, and now she rejoiced. She had despaired about her life, and now she was ready to live again.

She ran to the prophet and said to him, "Elisha, look what has happened; God has met our needs. What do you want me to do now that the jars are full?"

Elisha said to her, "Go, sell the oil and pay your debts" (v. 7).

There is a practical side to the miracle. The woman had to collect the pots. She also had to pour the oil. Eventually she had to enter a business transaction to negotiate a market price to sell the oil, pay the debts, and see her sons freed and fed. And so it is with us—we must also be practical and proactive; let us look around at what we *do* have, however inconsequential it may seem, and expect to see how God will use whatever we bring to him.

God knew how much oil the woman and her sons needed to live, but forever they would live with the memory of crying out to God and having been heard.

The whole community became a picture of the extraordinary grace of God. This wasn't a private matter; every person who had loaned a vessel saw that it was full to overflowing. The community saw God in their midst.

Sometimes we are in the position of the prophet's widow, crying out to God. Sometimes we are in the position of the community members, who were asked if they had any jars to give. The woman would eventually sell the oil; they might not get their jars back. If others are to experience God's blessing, we may have to spot the needs of our neighbors, to give money or time, and even to sacrifice something of our own.

Like the prophet's widow, we may think we have nothing. Like the neighbors, perhaps we think we have little to give. We may wish our circumstances were different. But God can use—and multiply—what little we have if we are willing to let him, and if we are willing to operate as a sacrificing and others-centered community. We cannot give what we haven't got. But what we do have, however small, God can use.

In this story, the woman needed money, but our needs may be very different; they may not be financial. Take but one example of real emotional need: the pervading loneliness that continues to grow in our societies, not only among the older generation but also in the younger generation for whom social media has turned out to be anything but social in terms of creating real relationships and community. Even if we only have a spare hour a week, if we were to invest that time in visiting a lonely neighbor or a vulnerable friend, God can multiply it for enormous blessing, both to the recipient and the giver of that time.

At times, we find ourselves crying out to God for our own needs—and at times we hear God's call in the needs of others. Their needs may be for something practical like the jars, or their needs may be for encouragement. We can be the ones who draw out the callings of others when they are not confident enough to respond on their own or when they don't think they have any gifts to give. Or we can point to the things they do have that could grow into fruitful activities but which they, like the woman in the story, have disregarded because they seem too small or apparently unexceptional.

Perhaps God will use you to tell a friend what a great listener he is, or a neighbor how entrepreneurial she is, or a coworker what a great problem-solver he is. For many reasons, our own talents can be screened from us, and often a word from a friend or colleague can unlock a treasure chest of hidden gems. Of all the ministries I get involved in, I love nothing more than using a gift God has given me to notice the unseen giftings in others and to speak life into them.

USING OUR TALENTS

We can learn a good deal about using what we have been given from the parable of the talents—or the parable of the minas—as told by Jesus in Luke's gospel.

A man of noble birth went to a distant country to have himself appointed king and then to return. So he called ten of his servants and gave them ten minas. "Put this money to work," he said, "until I come back."

But his subjects hated him and sent a delegation after him to say, "We don't want this man to be our king."

He was made king, however, and returned home. Then he sent for the servants to whom he had given the money, in order to find out what they had gained with it.

The first one came and said, "Sir, your mina has earned ten more."

"Well done, my good servant!" his master replied. "Because you have been trustworthy in a very small matter, take charge of ten cities."

The second came and said, "Sir, your mina has earned five more."

His master answered, "You take charge of five cities."

Then another servant came and said, "Sir, here is your mina; I have kept it laid away in a piece of cloth. I was afraid of you, because you are a hard man. You take out what you did not put in and reap what you did not sow."

His master replied, "I will judge you by your own words, you wicked servant! You knew, did you, that I am a hard man, taking out what I did not put in, and reaping what I did not sow? Why then didn't you put my money on deposit, so that when I came back, I could have collected it with interest?"

Then he said to those standing by, "Take his mina away from him and give it to the one who has ten minas."

"Sir," they said, "he already has ten!"

He replied, "I tell you that to everyone who has, more will be given, but as for the one who has nothing, even what they have will be taken away." (Luke 19:12–26)

This is a gritty parable. No punches are pulled. It addresses money but only as a powerful vehicle for the story. Specifically, it deals with the way in which people approach the *gifts* that have been given to them. It is revolutionary stuff. Jesus used this parable

CALLED TO FLOURISH

deliberately to challenge the prevailing Greek worldview at the time, which was that work should not be done by respectable people. Leisure, contemplation, and enjoyment were the touchstones of the fulfilled life. Jesus turned this idea on its head. He talked about work, investment, risk, performance-based returns, and differentiation based on ability (not everyone was given the same number of talents).

Jesus wants us to consider how we use *all that we have*—our giftings, relationships, imaginations, time, energies, and money. God gives us all different gifts with which to fulfill our callings. This isn't a human version of GoCompare.com, inviting us to compare ourselves to others. Comparing is futile, competing is frustrating, but receiving customized gifts and using them brings fulfillment.

Bruce repeatedly tells me that he enjoys work, is good at his job, and is well rewarded. But he struggles with "comparititis." He simply cannot break the need to run a checklist of how he is doing relative to others. And this is debilitating, for the very obvious reason that there is nothing he can do about the gifting of others. And it hits him hard, as he has to face the fact that he is who he is and cannot change the hand he has been dealt. I have urged him to see himself complete as he is, with a unique calling. God wonderfully makes each of us with a distinct life calling. It really is a question of *what I will do with what I have* rather than *what I might be able to do if I were different.*

Having said that, it is right to ask ourselves whether we're really firing on all cylinders or whether we're just doing enough to get by. Perhaps we are doing enough for nobody to comment or to criticize, or just enough to feel satisfied about what we're doing. But Jesus came to give us life, so we would "have it abundantly" (John 10:10 ESV).

I remember a stinging rebuke given to me by a wise adviser. We were talking about what I was doing and the many activities I was involved in. When he challenged me about the quality of these

55

various achievements, he said, "You have done well, and anyone around you will be telling you how well you have been doing, but what do *you* say about the intensity of play? Are you really focused and using what you have to the best advantage, or are you skimming by, growing wider but not deeper? In fact, you can congratulate yourself on satisfactory *under*performance. You are satisfied, and almost everyone else would believe that you had performed to a very high standard. But in your heart of hearts, you know that you could do better with what you have."

Satisfactory underperformance. Ouch! It stings even now.

GROWING IN OBEDIENCE

In Acts 9, we read about Ananias, who was somewhat terrified to be called on by God to go and speak to Saul just after an encounter with the risen Lord had blinded him. Ananias was given a small, simple task—but one that had momentous consequences. He was the person called to speak the words of encouragement that initiated the ministry of the man who would soon be known as Paul.

Ananias is known merely as a disciple. This could be you or me. And we see him respond as so often we do. We recognize God's call and say yes (v. 10). But then the excuses grow with a string of "buts." In his case, he rightly pointed out that Saul was a member of a violent religious police force not dissimilar to those operated by Daesh or the Taliban today. What a task to be asked to encourage *him*! Ananias said, "But" (as we often do)—and the Lord said, "Go!"

Ananias was obedient. He went to Saul as a messenger, called out of him the anointing that God had on his life, and saw him filled with the Spirit.

When Ananias entered the house, he laid hands on Saul. Saul was blind, so Ananias's touch must have meant a great deal to him. We should not underestimate the huge message that a hug or a hand on a shoulder conveys. His gesture was accompanied by two of the most reconciling words in Scripture: "Brother Saul" (v. 17). The sense of warmth and familial closeness of "brother" conflicts with "Saul," the name of an archenemy and persecutor of Christians. The violent religious extremist and the brother in Christ meet. In uniting these two words, "Brother Saul," Ananias demonstrated a level of acceptance and encouragement from which he could speak into Saul's life and affirm him as a chosen instrument of God. This was a small act of obedience by Ananias, but one with a massive result. A life was turned around, a calling confirmed, and the ministry of one of the greatest men in history was launched.

How true this is for you and for me as we look to encourage friends to step into their callings. Any of us can do this. Like Ananias, we simply need to be obedient to God's prompting. I am so grateful to those who have taken the risks and stepped out in faith with a word of encouragement, particularly at times when my calling has seemed to play at a pitch so low as to be almost inaudible.

God has endowed us with a particular suite of gifts: intellect, emotion, skill, and intuition. They are what we need to perform our callings in the world. We do not have to compete with what we see in others in order to be fulfilled at work and in our callings. All I need is to be me. I cannot fulfill someone else's passion. Ananias was the supporting role to Saul's lead, but he was essential to the story of Saul's conversion, just as the widow's community was essential in their provision of the jars, without which God could not have acted as he did. God needs us all. Lead roles, supporting roles, background roles—all are equally important to God and are used by him. We can take different roles in different situations. Even the donkey in the nativity story plays a critical role—without it, Mary and Joseph may never have made it to Bethlehem!

How much do we need to hear this message today? A young pastor at a large church once told me that he was nothing more than a cog in a machine. He didn't feel that he made any real contribution to the outcome of the ministry of the church. And it's not just junior pastors who are insecure. So many people get frustrated at work because they think they are just going through the motions in the background, never impacting the big decisions.

What my young pastor friend needed to remember—what we all need to remember—is that cogs play an essential role in mechanics. Without them the wheels never turn. Indeed, there's a sense in which all of us are "just" cogs in a bigger machine, no matter our worldly status. We shouldn't be afraid of playing a supporting role. Remember that divine perspective? The world might see the supporting cast as inferior, but God values the role of every participant.

The great women and men who changed history could never have achieved what they did on their own. They may be the figureheads, but the real change comes through *the body of people* who each lend his or her individual efforts. Martin Luther King Jr. marching to Selma alone would have been useless. Nelson Mandela would have been left in jail to rot if it hadn't been for the support of countless others keeping his vision alive, lobbying and demonstrating outside Trafalgar Square and the major capitals of the world. The human genome could never have been mapped by a single scientist. We need to step back and see the big picture—our small offerings can collectively support huge changes.

To see ourselves as cogs in a machine is not to demean ourselves but to acknowledge the need for collective action. Let us not forget that Lionel Messi—the greatest soccer player of his age—would not be able to dazzle his fans without the team spirit of his Barcelona colleagues. As we come to understand the collective might of small contributions, we can be released from the individualistic anxiety that comes with comparing ourselves to others.

Plant a Seed

In Luke 13, Jesus described what the kingdom of God is like: "It is like a mustard seed, which a man took and planted in his garden.

It grew and became a tree, and the birds perched in its branches"
(v. 19). The mustard seed is as small a seed as can be found. But it
grows into a big tree. Jesus was making the point that small acts can
have large results. Our callings are like this; they may start with a
small thought, a suggestion from someone about what we can do
with our lives. But the crucial image is that we "*took* and *planted* in
[our] garden."

Often we spend time looking at the seed—that is, the calling—
looking at the seed packet, wondering where exactly we should plant
it, dreaming about how big it might grow. But we have to take it out
of the packet and plant it. No seed will germinate and grow until it
is planted. That sounds so obvious. But we should never be afraid
of the obvious. Opportunity may be right under our noses, but we
miss it.

Jesus told us that the man plants the seed "in his garden." We
are called to take the small steps close to home. Sometimes we
think we need to take giant steps in far-flung places, when in fact,
as was the case in the parable, we are called to plant in our own
backyards—the place we know best.

My wife, Fi, is a talented musician. It is a gift that God has given
her. She also has a heart for older people. Much time and energy is
given to the young—and rightly so—but Fi loves to reach out to the
older generation. Several years ago, she decided that she wanted to
do something to minister to them. And what she did was incredibly
simple. She invited a number of older people to our home, gave them
tea, and played the piano for them. That's all. Small and simple.
The letters she received after her first "concert" were so moving that
she determined to see that dream grow a little larger.

Now, six times a year, if you go to our church in Onslow Square,
London, you will hear a classical concert of the most amazing
kind, attended by four or five hundred older people. For many of
them—often lonely and sometimes lacking anything to look forward to—these concerts are a highlight. An outreach team makes

sandwiches and serves a formal tea to the guests. Fi plays the piano, and some of the most talented musicians in London give their free time to perform. The standard is equal to that of any major concert hall in the country.

Her small idea, which began by embracing the gift she had been given, was multiplied and expanded by our generous God. Let us not bury our gifts; our gifts don't just serve our own needs for fulfillment; they have a wider purpose to influence, inspire, encourage, and bless those around us.

None of us are perfect; all of us have blind spots or weaknesses. But these failings only hold us back if we think they prevent God from using us.

When Jesus fed the five thousand (John 6:1–15), it was a small boy's meal that was multiplied. Just imagine if the boy hadn't been prepared to give to Jesus his small basket of bread and fish. Imagine if the boy had held back his offering, grasping it tightly so that no one could take from him what precious food he had, assuming that he was just a boy with nothing to offer. There would have been no miracle. Five thousand people would have gone hungry, and Jesus might not have demonstrated his extraordinary provision and generosity. What we have, however small, we must keep giving to the Lord for his miraculous purposes. The boy was obedient, and God honored him.

Don't let the people around you constrain your calling by their views of you. Only you know the gifts that God has given to you. Calling and gifting run together. The question is, will you be intentional about using them?

Let us remember that the economy of the kingdom of God is based not on power but on potential. So many of the biblical heroes were reluctant to step into their callings because they didn't believe they could ever amount to anything significant.

When God called Moses to free the Israelites, Moses protested that he could not speak publicly. When Sarah was promised a son, she protested that she was too old; and when Jeremiah was told to prophesy, he protested that he was too young. When God sent Gideon to fight the Midianites, Gideon protested that his family was insignificant. When Samuel anointed Saul with oil, Saul protested that his tribe was too small, and when Samuel anointed David, Jesse protested that David was the youngest of eight sons. Even Mary, when she was promised that she would carry the Messiah, protested that she was a virgin (although we probably can't begrudge her that one!).

I wonder if you can recognize yourself in any of these biblical heroes. I certainly can. What encouragement!

Using what we have been given (however small), encouraging others to use their gifts, and being obedient to that heavenly calling are vital. So many people are afraid to answer their callings because they feel too old or too young, not cool enough or smart enough or important enough to be of use to God. But with God, our seemingly insignificant contributions can make a significant impact. Our small actions can have big consequences.

In 1998, Jo Rice was working at Alpha (a ten-week course that introduces the basics of Christianity), putting together a mailing with some of the young people at Huntercombe Young Offenders Institution (YOI). She was sitting around a table with a selection of young inmates who had volunteered to help stuff envelopes. Tyrone was next to her, and he did not give her an easy few days. He questioned her incessantly about Christianity: "But why do bad things happen if God is meant to be so good?" "Is it true you can't have sex before marriage?" "What is the whole deal with heaven anyway?" The questions were relentless. And to every answer she gave, he had a witty reply that left Jo searching for words. After several hours of this, Jo said, "*Please stop!* I'm exhausted. You are too clever for me— the way you can spin an argument is too good. Can't we just talk about last night's television?"

Tyrone looked shocked. It was clear that no one had ever told him he was clever. It was like a revelation to him, and his demeanor changed instantly. His defenses came down, and when Jo got back to the office, she returned to find a letter and a photo from Tyrone asking her to correspond with him.

On her way home, Jo reflected on this small encounter and wondered whether working with disadvantaged young people might not be as complicated as everyone seemed to think. *Could it actually be really simple? A specific encouragement, a few words of affirmation—could this be the start of helping young people from difficult backgrounds turn their lives around?* Inside, a seed was sown. She prayed that God would help her to find expression for this idea. A few months later she sat next to a friend, Tom Jackson, at a wedding. He talked passionately about an idea he had to see disadvantaged young people equipped with life skills and encouraged into employment. *Bam!* There it was. A chance for her idea to meet with Tom's. Twelve years later, Spear is a thriving initiative that partners with local churches to run coaching programs for unemployed young people from disadvantaged backgrounds.

One small comment to encourage a young man, and a seed was sown. My prayer is that we, too, might have the courage to sow small seeds. We will be amazed at what great works God can grow out of the smallest ideas and dreams.

FOUR

CALLED TO WAIT

LIFE HAS SEASONS. FROM THE BEGINNING OF THE BIBLE IN Genesis 1, we see the Creator God at work: "Separate Day from Night. Mark seasons and days and years" (v. 14 THE MESSAGE). Each of these seasons has a different character. In a rapidly changing world, we all face new seasons in our lives, some we choose and others that are forced upon us: one stage of life ends for another to begin; new career challenges lead to different jobs; new opportunities change our ways of living.

There are times when we are called to prepare for these new seasons. This is the game before the game. It is as if we are in training but the game schedule is not yet out and we don't know the date or the time of the match. This game before the game is an essential part of our calling as Christians. It is often a neglected time of preparation, which should be taken much more seriously by those who want to be ready and equipped—mentally, physically, spiritually, and emotionally—to take on the next task or calling.

How then do we prepare ourselves? Discovering a calling is not like doing a Google search; it does not happen in an instant. We need to be intentional about taking action rather than just waiting for our callings to drop into our laps.

TIME IN THE WAITING ROOM

You probably know the feeling: Your mind begins to wander away from the familiar place where you have been working when a new and unexpected opportunity develops an increasingly strong life of its own as the idea grows. But somehow you know that you have to wait to see whether this is a real, new calling or just a scratchy reaction to tiresome people and seemingly endless problems at work. Waiting is bad enough for an activist. Waiting *patiently* is nigh impossible! But that is what the psalmist said repeatedly: "I waited patiently for the LORD" (Psalm 40:1). Waiting is a part of the spiritual discipline essential to everyone who is following Jesus. But then, significantly, the psalmist added, "he turned to me and heard my cry." I have found the first part—waiting—almost unbearable at times. Yet when I have clung to that second half of the promise, I have not been disappointed.

What do you do in the waiting room? Fill in the doctor's forms, give your history, and then wait to be called while flicking through last month's magazines. Every now and then you pop up to see whether you have slipped off the list or how long it will take for the doctor to see you.

Waiting is so very hard. But unlike the doctor's waiting room, God's waiting rooms are *part of the consultation*. It matters to him that we are prepared before we hear from him. Taking time to get ready is therefore not an annoying interlude but an essential ingredient and part of his equipping.

We begin to dream of what might be. We have a sense that the ties to our current circumstances are being loosened and something different is beginning. God allows conviction to grow out of our initial dreams and impressions, but this takes time. Waiting is a kind of spiritual workshop. But how do we deal with this maddening delay? What do we do when we can't do anything? And how do we keep the dream alive when we can't yet live the dream?

When we are stressed because we cannot lay hold of what we really want, it is easy to start comparing ourselves with others who appear to be flourishing in their dreams. And this only fuels our desire for something to happen and reminds us of what could be but isn't yet—or worse, might not ever be. In these times, we have a tendency to believe that nothing good will come from this experience of waiting. But this is the most valuable time of our lives in Christ: when he draws near and works with us to align our wills to his purpose. This season enables us to respond to his call for the next phase of our lives. There is excitement in this time if we have the right attitude and if we can embrace rather than resist the challenges of the season.

It can be painful maintaining this holding pattern. It is bad enough in a stack above Heathrow Airport, circling the runway, waiting for a slot to free up in order to land. It seems so pointless. But we don't always see the big picture. By our judgment, we should land. But air traffic control sees the bigger picture, and not just one airplane full of frustrated passengers. Other factors must be considered to get the right timing for the landing: other planes might have first priority and runways have to be available. We do not see the context surrounding our individual circumstances. We are required to trust Jesus for the timing.

God has bound himself to act within the framework of time. When he acted in creation, he did so consciously—limiting eternity to the restrictions of a time-based world. Time unfolds according to his will, and, as has often been observed, he is seldom early but never late. So waiting is programmed into the very operation system of God's plan for humanity. And our comfort is that we cannot beat him by bringing into existence a change of circumstance of our own. We are often tempted to try and do more than we are called to do, but we cannot do more than he has planned for us.

Abraham waited twenty-five years for his life's calling to be fulfilled. Moses waited forty years, and, ultimately, Jesus waited thirty years to begin his main ministry. As the saying goes, "If God is making you wait, you are in good company!" By comparison, the six months or one year of champing at the bit seems less significant.

Dreams take time to be fulfilled. There is an inner game that has to be played out before we can face the outer one. Our mindsets and foci need to be strengthened first. Every athlete knows the importance of this pre-match prep. Michael Jordan was quite clear: "You have to expect things of yourself before you can do them."[1] This is what happens in the waiting time. The process of preparing is as important as the plan.

Gary Mack, the author of *Mind Gym*, tells the story of Pelé, the legendary Brazilian soccer player.[2] Pelé told Mack about his routine the day of a match. He would arrive about an hour before and find an isolated, quiet place to lie down and place a pillow over his eyes. From there, Pelé would watch a film in his "mind's eye." He began playing the movie in his head, starting from playing soccer on the beaches of Brazil as a child, where he could feel the hot sun on his back, the ocean breeze in the background. He would vividly recall the thrill the game brought him. Pelé would immerse himself in his love of soccer and relive those wonderful memories.

From there, Pelé would relive his greatest moments on the world stage. He talked about letting himself feel and enjoy the intensity of these moments, the thrill of winning over and over again. He spoke about the importance of making a strong connection to his past before he could begin thinking about the current event. Pelé would then begin the final installment in his film by seeing himself *as he was about to become*: scoring goals, flying past defenders, playing brilliantly. He made a movie of positive images that brought strong feelings of enjoyment and success.

This is perhaps the most important thing for us to take away and apply to our own performance preparation. Pelé would imagine everything *before* it happened: the crowd, the field, his team, his opponents, the atmosphere—every element of what he was about to experience—always holding on to those strong emotional positive images of success. He imagined himself performing like an irresistible force that could not be stopped. Then he would begin his stretching and exercise routine and head into the stadium, mentally and physically unstoppable.

In biblical stories, the pattern is similar but distinctive. God often plants dreams and visions in us before they happen. God changed Abram's name to Abraham, which meant "father of nations, or multitude," *before* he had the promised child. This was the means he used to convince Abraham to call for what he did not yet have in reality. God had established the future by promise, but Abraham had to call it into reality by mixing faith with God's Word. Every time he said, "I am Abraham," he was declaring the promise that was not yet manifest (see Romans 4:17).

I have a friend named Robert who has a prophetic gift. He has a friend in the army, James, who year after year failed to get promoted from major to lieutenant colonel. He was missing the promotion by tiny margins of one or two points. James was beginning to get despondent and started to talk about leaving the army altogether. Robert felt strongly that the army was God's calling for James, so every time he sent James a text message he called him "Colonel." For two years Robert used this nickname, until finally James called him with the great news that he had at last been promoted. What Robert did was an act of encouragement. It was not just a wishful thought but a belief that, after the waiting period, God would respond. It was an act of faith and a reminder of what was yet to be.

I do not mean that you should go around proclaiming, "I shall be the next president of the United States," but there is a sense, as with Pelé, of *visualizing* with faith and prayer a version of your future that fits your wiring as a person, your gifting and experience, and also God's abundant goodness and promises. It wouldn't be crass to sum it up as the "power of positive thinking," provided we realize that both the source of our hope and our ability to deliver come from the Holy Spirit. We need to be firm, positive, and inspired to believe the promises of the Bible, as did David in Psalm 118, who said with determination, "I shall not die, but live, and declare the works of the LORD" (v. 17 NKJV).

My own experience of this waiting time has been more difficult in reality than in the theory I have presented. For me waiting is a nightmare, and I can feel overwhelmed by frustration. I find myself crying out with the psalmist, "How long, LORD?" (Psalm 13:1), and wondering why I can't get going when everything appears to be in place.

It may be helpful to give a few pointers of how I have tried to deal with the times when my own dreams and hopes have been deferred or denied me altogether.

TEN WINNING WAYS IN THE WAITING ROOM

1. WAIT WITH PERSISTENCE

Sometimes the task for which we are being prepared has not yet been fully disclosed to us. And the more demanding the new calling, the tougher the preparation might be. I have often reminded myself of the story of the persistent widow, who relentlessly pursued the judge for the outcome she dreamed of, until he finally granted the request (Luke 18:1–8). This story inspires us to labor in prayer to see our dreams fulfilled.

2. REMEMBER GOD IS IN CONTROL

So often the pain of uncertainty and anxiety, which accompanies major shifts in our lives, is so overwhelming that we assume it must be the devil's work, perhaps a deliberate and targeted attack to unsettle us in our callings. It usually isn't. All we need to remember in these times are four words: *God is with us*. This is the declaration—"Immanuel, God with us" (Matthew 1:23)—that starts Matthew's gospel and indeed ends it: "And surely I am with you always, to the very end of the age" (Matthew 28:20). He knows and he cares. He is preparing. He may be silent, but he is not absent.

3. EMBRACE THE CHANGE

Don't resist it—and believe good will come of the waiting. Doubts may emerge, but they need not stay. Entertaining doubt for too long gives it undeserved legitimacy. When Moses was called, he hung back and raised one excuse after another: "Who am I that I should go to Pharaoh?" (Exodus 3:11) and "What if they do not believe me or listen to me?" (Exodus 4:1) and "I am slow of speech and tongue. . . . Please send someone else" (vv. 10, 13). Our own feelings of inadequacy or weakness are always answered by God's presence and strength: "As I was with Moses, so I will be with you; I will never leave you nor forsake you" (Joshua 1:5).

4. AVOID FEELING ALONE

In his most depressed moment, Elijah complained to God that he was the only one going through this time of waiting for God to act, the only one taking on the priests and the followers of Baal: "The people of Israel have forsaken your covenant, thrown down your altars, and killed your prophets with the sword, and I, even I only, am left, and they seek my life, to take it away" (1 Kings 19:14 ESV). Elijah, of course, was not alone, and when God sent him back to Ahab, he revealed that there were seven thousand others in Israel who had refused to bow to the Baals. However alone we feel, there are others going through the same times of transition, feeling the same disorientation, lacking the same assurance, and struggling just as hard. It is small comfort to know that we are not left alone, but it is still worth remembering that we join every person of God, in every age, who has had to learn this fundamental lesson: waiting on God is the first and greatest test of our trust in him.

5. LIVE IN THE PRESENT

We shouldn't settle down in the waiting room to relive the past. The past is no guide to the future. Sometimes it is helpful to reflect, but we also need to clear the decks of past disappointments, frustrations, and mistakes. It is a choice to say with the psalmist, "*This is the day the LORD has made*; We will rejoice and be glad in it" (Psalm 118:24 NKJV, emphasis added). The day is new and fresh: "his compassions never fail. They are new every morning" (Lamentations 3:22–23). Replaying the action is tempting, but the past is unrepeatable. New circumstances, new skills, and new relationships make each day a unique day for the Lord to nudge us on to better play.

6. DON'T STRESS ABOUT THE EXIT

While we are in the waiting room, there is no point stressing about the exit. It will come in its time. Just as Joseph had to go through time in prison, so we may well have to stay expectant in a trying and unsettling place. The timing belongs to God. It is noteworthy that Joseph was not idle in prison. In fact, he had the opportunity to exercise his gift of prophecy, which two years later resulted in his release from his very demanding waiting room and his promotion to prime minister of Egypt. Likewise, Joshua was required to march seven times around the city of Jericho before taking the city (Joshua 6). Our work of preparation may be of a spiritual or practical nature—it tends to be a mixture of both—but there is always plenty we can do as we wait.

7. DON'T RUSH AHEAD

My father was a farmer who grew fruit. Whenever we impatiently tested the green avocados, he would remind me that you can't squeeze a fruit ripe. It ripens in its season. Sometimes it seems such a long time for the harvest to come. It is the same with God's seasons—we cannot accelerate them, as God reminds us in Isaiah 60:22: "I am the LORD; in its time I will do this swiftly." And every effort of our own to accelerate God's plan will merely bear inedible green fruit. Remember in Psalm 1: the person who delights in the Word of God "is like a tree planted by streams of water, which yields its fruit in season" (v. 3). Rushing is not biblical. In our culture where speed is the ideal, let us dare to slow the pace and trust God's timing.

I once asked Michael, a friend in his early twenties, what distinguished the attitudes of him and his friends from the attitude of his parents' generation. He had several answers, and then, as his parting comment, he said, "I think we all want shortcuts. We have become so used to finding short, efficient ways to use computers without having to go through long processes. We hate waiting. And we have been helped by the programmers who make it easier to take shortcuts without having to go through labor-intensive actions. We love one-click applications. Press Cmd+A, and all the text is highlighted without having to go through it line by line."

Sadly, spiritual shortcuts don't work. There isn't an efficient way to fast-track the waiting time. Whenever I have tried to take a shortcut in spiritual growth, I have come up short. The path always leads us back to the tried and challenging ways of waiting for the Lord.

8. STICK WITH THE LITTLE THINGS

While we wait, we need to keep going with our daily tasks—giving to our core relationships, being engaged in our communities, getting on with life—until it is clear that it is time to move. And when we work, we work graciously, not grudgingly, for Christ is the real Master we serve whenever and wherever. Remember the old proverb: while I wait he is working, while I work he is waiting! There is enough of a truth there to be worth remembering.

9. DRAW CLOSE TO GOD

God uses these times of waiting to draw us closer to him, to ourselves, and to our loved ones. So many people have told me that in this time of uncertainty they have drawn closer to not only God but also their spouses and others near them. In the battle for our attention, God often has to let us go through a period of adversity so that we might attune our ears to his voice and discern his direction. In a frenzied world we often slot God into overactive lives, trying to force him to fit around our routines. This never works. A waiting period is a time to recognize that we have drifted into a world of expectation and instant answers. This is not the real world. Often God's way is to waken within us a calling, but then to allow us to recognize that his greatest desire is to draw close to us.

In the book of Isaiah, King Hezekiah fell ill and received word from the prophet Amos that he was about to die. The king cried out to God for salvation, and after a short period of waiting, God sent Isaiah to inform him that he would now live. Unsurprisingly, the king was fairly relieved! But even before he was cured, King Hezekiah started singing a song of praise to the Lord, which contains these lines:

> But what can I say?
>> He has spoken to me, and he himself has done this.
> I will walk humbly all my years
>> because of this anguish of my soul.
> Lord, by such things people live;
>> and my spirit finds life in them too.
> You restored me to health
>> and let me live.
> Surely it was for my benefit
>> that I suffered such anguish.
> In your love you kept me
>> from the pit of destruction;
> you have put all my sins
>> behind your back. (Isaiah 38:15–17)

In the darkness of his uncertainty, Hezekiah found himself drawn close to God—able to appreciate afresh the grace and love of his Savior.

10. FIND WORTH IN THE WAITING

The process of being reoriented is as important as the planned outcome. We are strengthened by the knowledge that what we do today is valuable for tomorrow. Our cry is, "How long?" but God's cry is, "You can trust me." Our dreams are often given and then delayed in order to be sure that we rest in him and see the fulfillment of these dreams as having come from him.

Success very often comes from this season of preparation. But it needs to be followed by a strategy to get the job done. When the preparation phase is over, it is time to get up and go!

DETERMINED DREAMING

Waiting can be so hard. Many of us know all too well the sinking feeling in the pit of our stomachs when forces outside our control conspire to put our dreams on hold. In the words of the writer of the Proverbs, "Hope deferred makes the heart sick." Yet the next line is the hope that we cling to: "but a longing fulfilled is a tree of life" (Proverbs 13:12). Dreams are not just fantastical diversions in our lives, but the very stuff of living. And they matter to God.

The essence of a dream is prospective, an aspiration to transcend what is not yet attained. John Stott, one of the leading biblical writers of the twentieth century, is said to have described visionary dreaming as "a deep dissatisfaction of what *is* and a clear grasp of what *could be*."[3] Visionary dreaming has to go beyond discontent to see how things could actually be different. How, in practice, can the deep malaise that we perceive be made whole again through the light of Christ?

For many years my greatest dissatisfaction has been that the younger generation seems to have lost its spiritual center. So many people are listless, uncertain, and wavering in their spiritual lives, overwhelmed by a plethora of options. Choice, which once was a blessing to be fought for, has become a curse. I long to see these young people filled with energy and passion and a purpose that comes from God, all of which will change their lives and the lives of those around them. My dissatisfaction has been easy to spot. It has colored my life. But it has been much harder to achieve a vision or dream for *how* things could be transformed. For many years I prayed to God to give me such a vision, that I might begin to see how I could play a role in building up this generation.

Over the years that I have prayed this prayer, God has led me in many different ventures. One of the first started with me drawing together a group of young leaders to a gathering called READY, aimed at seeing a new generation released and raised up. I started the event in order to help equip young men and women who were struggling with the concept that God might be interested in their lives outside of church. Martin Smith and Matt Redman led our worship—what exciting times! One evening Matt asked whether he could sing a new song about King David dancing before the ark of the covenant until his clothes fell off, leading David to tell his embarrassed wife, Michal, "I will become even more undignified than this" (2 Samuel 6:22). So enthusiastic was his worship that I became seriously concerned that an overzealous Matt might begin to strip off his clothes in a fit of realistic biblical simulation!

The needs of the younger generation have, if anything, grown since that first venture. Many other great gatherings have sprung up—New Wine and Momentum in the United Kingdom, and Passion in the United States. Yet still I sensed an unmet need when it came to equipping and empowering those in their twenties and thirties with the biblical leadership skills to be effective at work and to dream with determination. And so out of my dissatisfaction God grew a new dream—to create a place where young Christians could receive leadership training to help them lead others in all areas of their lives. Nicky Gumbel, the leader of my church in London, saw this need and made the necessary resources available for the program to grow. It has taken a long time for the Leadership College to take form and offer specific training in leadership for those in the workplace, but it has been well worth the wait!

Dissatisfaction, dreams, destiny. Each one leads to the next.

When we have dreams that we long to achieve, frequently they are given in one season but fulfilled in another. We have to have *determined* dreams, not daydreams, if we are to fulfill all that God calls us to.

It is important that dreams and determination run together, in order to separate our frivolous fantasies from our God-given ambitions. I have noticed over the years that people fail not because of a lack of dreams but because of a lack of determination. It can be difficult to endure the tediousness of the waiting room, and those who lack the determination to see it through can often walk out in frustration. Determined dreaming is not the listless daydreaming where we gaze into the middle distance, imagining a better world. That's all very well, but nothing will happen, and the daydream will evaporate as soon as the real world strikes and the going gets tough. We need to engage our wills and commitment. To fulfill our destiny, we require determination and discernment.

There is an inspiring group of young men in our church who are passionate about sharpening their skills for God. A few years ago they listened to Gary Haugen, CEO of the International Justice Mission, speak on human trafficking and the scourge of this worldwide evil. They were struck by what they heard and motivated to do something about it. They began to ask, "How can we allow trafficking of human beings in our age and in our city?"

They started praying together during Tuesday lunchtimes every week for six months, gathering a few people around them.

Theirs was a bold dream. But ours is a big God. And so they pressed on, waiting, dreaming, and praying about all the practical issues that they would have to address if they were to take real action against modern-day slavery. They were sure there was *something* God was calling them into, but the way ahead wasn't clear. So they pressed into their dream, bringing it before God again and again.

After six months of determined dreaming, God was showing them a way forward. They decided they needed to get the best research available to show what was actually happening on our streets, in the very heart of London. They pooled their money to start a campaign. The first step was to commission expert analysts to gather the facts. They then took the report to the government and lobbied for a change in the law to prevent this evil practice from continuing in our country. The report was well received, and the government considered their arguments. As a result of their prayers, financial commitment, and research, the Modern Slavery Act came to life as a law in the United Kingdom.

They dreamed. They dared. They were determined, and they delivered. But they had to go through the waiting room—the game before the game. They needed to remain determined through that period of waiting, listening, and discerning the heart and will of God. And in that waiting, they were strengthened and prepared for the challenges ahead.

As followers of Christ, we must not be disheartened by the constant stream of bad news that flows out of news broadcasts. Just as Paul said in his letter to the Philippians, so must we "press on, that I may lay hold of that for which Christ Jesus has also laid hold of me" (Philippians 3:12 NKJV). Let us not stand idle but be gripped by the future and by what—in God's power—could be.

In his memorable "I Have a Dream" speech, Martin Luther King Jr. spoke of his dream of racial justice in the United States and worldwide. He was absolutely determined to see it come alive. But there must have been plenty of times in his life when King felt stuck in the waiting room—in the game before the game. With much of the US political establishment arrayed against the civil rights movement, and with FBI director J. Edgar Hoover harboring a personal hatred for him, there were countless moments when the path to that dream seemed hopelessly blocked. How easy it would have been to resign himself to the status quo and to leave the fight for equality to someone else.

But King was determined in his dreaming. He knew he had a calling from God, and he refused to let that dream fizzle and die, even when it seemed impossible.

In the Bible, we read of another king who found his calling apparently blocked by the might of the political establishment. In 1 Samuel 16, we see the teenaged boy David, youngest of eight brothers, anointed by the prophet Samuel as the next king of Israel. But it was perhaps fifteen long years before David was able to ascend the throne and fulfill the destiny God had laid out for him. There were times in the wilderness when David—oppressed, exiled, and ruthlessly hunted by King Saul—questioned whether this had all been a huge mistake. There were times when he wondered if he had been forgotten, if God would ever fulfill the promises that he had made.

Psalm 13, it seems, was written at just such a time.

> How long, LORD? Will you forget me forever?
>> How long will you hide your face from me?
> How long must I wrestle with my thoughts
>> and day after day have sorrow in my heart?
>> How long will my enemy triumph over me?
>
> Look on me and answer, LORD my God.
>> Give light to my eyes, or I will sleep in death,
> and my enemy will say, "I have overcome him,"
>> and my foes will rejoice when I fall. (vv. 1–4)

But David didn't stop there. Despite his questions, his repeated cry of "how long?" he clung to the calling that he had been given, and to the faithfulness of God.

> But I trust in your unfailing love;
>> my heart rejoices in your salvation.
> I will sing the LORD's praise,
>> for he has been good to me." (vv. 5–6)

DON'T CUT CORNERS

The story of David is a great lesson for us today. His trust in God kept him steadfast in his calling throughout those periods of waiting in the wilderness. Whenever doubts came upon him or he questioned the calling that God had placed on his life, he chose to reaffirm the faithfulness of the Lord. This was his game before the game, a time of deep learning and maturing as he grew to trust in the promises of God.

But for David, trusting in God also meant trusting in the *ways* of God. We can learn a great lesson about what it means to wait *well* when we read 1 Samuel 24.

Saul, at the height of his reign and with three thousand men at his side, had hunted David and his band of followers into the desert. Things were looking pretty desperate for the son of Jesse when, in a sudden twist of fate, the king of Israel stopped to relieve himself in the very cave where David and his men were hiding!

David's men were overjoyed. "This is the day the LORD spoke of when he said to you, 'I will give your enemy into your hands for you to deal with as you wish'" (v. 4).

The temptation must have been acute. By then David was well known across Israel as Samuel's anointed. Killing the king would have made David the obvious successor. All David had to do was creep up behind Saul, kill the man who was so desperately trying to kill him, and receive the crown of Israel promised to him by God several years prior.

But David didn't do it. He wouldn't commit murder. He knew that wasn't the way of God. He knew that it wasn't the timing of God. He trusted that God would unblock the path to his calling in the right time and in the right way. To kill Saul in such cold-blooded fashion would be to take the crown in David's time and in David's way. It would not be a shortcut but a wrong turn.

How different the attitude of David is from the attitude of another Old Testament hero: Jacob, the son of Isaac and twin brother of Esau. Jacob's story is well known. While the twins were still in her womb, their mother, Rebekah, had been promised by the Lord that the older brother (Esau) would serve the younger (Jacob). Jacob was destined to inherit God's promise to Abraham.

But neither Jacob nor Rebekah trusted God to fulfill his promises in God's way and in God's time. They took it upon themselves, cruelly tricking the elderly Isaac into passing his blessing on to Jacob instead of the firstborn and heir, Esau. And then, because of his actions, Jacob had to flee. He spent decades away from his family home, farming for his uncle in the east, afraid to return to his mother and father and brother. It was only by God's grace that he eventually returned to claim the calling that God had laid on his life from birth.

It's similar to the story of Abraham, who slept with the slave girl Hagar rather than trust that God would provide him descendants through his wife (Genesis 16).

How tempting it can be for us to cut corners as Jacob and Abraham did, to rationalize that compromising our integrity is the only way to secure our God-given dreams. But God does not want us to compromise. God does not want liars, cheaters, or thieves. Trusting that God has called us into something means trusting that he will bring it to fruition in his way and in his time. When we try to force his hand—when we try to fulfill those dreams in our own way and our own strength—we will create further obstacles to following in the callings that God has given us.

Paul wrote at various points in his letters about running a *good* race. It's not simply about getting to the end, but about getting there with integrity. How we approach the game before the game—how we prepare—is integral to running such a race.

On September 24, 1988, the finalists of the men's 100-meter sprint lined up on the start-line at the Seoul Summer Olympics. The race that followed was one of the greatest Olympic moments of all time. Out of the starting blocks like a bullet, Canadian Ben Johnson posted a time of 9.79 seconds, which bested his own world record and smashed the Olympic record by more than 0.04 seconds. He was hailed as a hero for a full three days before everything came crashing down around him. After testing positive for anabolic steroids, Johnson was stripped of his gold medal and his world record and was banned for two years, with his reputation in tatters.[4]

Ben Johnson chose to spend the game before the game loading up on banned substances. He chose to prepare for the race in a way that undermined his on-track success. But we, like Paul, should desire to run a *good* race. When we get to the end of all things, will we be able to say with Paul, "I have fought the good fight, I have finished the race, I have kept the faith" (2 Timothy 4:7)? Will we be able to look back on those seasons of waiting, confident that we remained faithful to the calling of God?

Let us be like King David and like Paul, who spent the game before the game faithfully waiting on the Lord's timing, refusing to take the shortcuts the world offers. They believed that God would "be [their] guide even to the end" (Psalm 48:14). His calling on our lives remains strong, even as we wait.

—— FIVE ——

CALLED TO CHOOSE

MAKING LIFE CHOICES IS NEVER EASY. YOU LEAVE COLLEGE OR university, and you have to make some kind of choice about what happens next. Or you are midway through your career, facing a crossroads, and you think, you *sense*, God might be calling you to something new. Maybe you have been made redundant in a job you were wedded to for years, and you are confronted by a whole new series of questions about where to go next. And the rent bills keep on coming, so there is a degree of urgency to your situation. Or perhaps you have already found your calling, but you need to find a way to keep the flame alive and not to stagnate or run dry.

Of course, such choice is the privilege of the few, and we should always see it as such. But the speed of change in technology and the rapidly changing face of the workplace make choice at times frightening and overwhelming. It is almost as if we can't cope with the number of alternatives: stay where we are, take some time out and return to work, work from home or remotely, study further, change our jobs or the way of doing them, join with others in doing something new, move to something more "spiritual" or "meaningful," take a break from full-time volunteer work. The choices are dizzying.

But, in my experience, they are made significantly easier by the knowledge that God calls us and is there *to guide us*. God first. That is the place to start.

People sometimes say, "God gave us a brain, so shouldn't we just use it?" The answer is quite obviously yes. But a problem arises in the use of the word *just*. Human judgment alone is not, in my view, sufficient. It must run parallel to and entwined with a purposeful seeking after God.

Other people say, "God's in charge, so surely we'll end up where he wants us." Again, there's truth in this, but to argue that our concerns are irrelevant would suggest that we don't have any say in matters. Sometimes it is true that we receive callings from God that are given as commands. Jonah was going to Nineveh—by boat or by fish. God's intention was clear: it was up to Jonah to decide the mode of transport. But this is an exceptional calling. The Bible makes it clear that God gives us a choice—that he works with us, not just through us.

For the most part, we are given the freedom to seek God's ways and then to make choices. We do not operate independently from him, but neither are we puppets dancing on a string. Our personal callings are not commands but beckonings and promptings. We enter into them in partnership with God, making use of the opportunities that God presents to us and the passions that he has given us.

Pastor and author Steve Furtick delivered a message entitled "God's Will Is Whatever." He based his title on the liberating words in Paul's letter to the Colossians, "And *whatever you do*, whether in word or deed, do it all in the name of the Lord Jesus, giving thanks to God the Father through him" (Colossians 3:17, emphasis added). Furtick explained that whatever we do can actually become God's will when we do it God's way. In other words, wherever you are right now (assuming that you are walking closely with the Lord and what you are doing is neither immoral nor illegal) is where you are meant to be. Your calling is not in some elusive, otherworldly, unreachable place. Your calling is right here, right now. You are called to get on and live in the light of that calling.

It is easy to think, *If I don't make the right decision about which of the two job offers to accept, I may miss God's call.* Many behave as if the Christian life is merely a determinist track for us to follow or miss. *But God's sovereignty never extinguishes the freedom he gives us to choose.* Within the context of God's great love for us, and our obeying of his commands, he allows us to roam freely and to make the decisions that are ours to make. This is true liberty born out of a continuing relationship with him.

It is for this reason that I find little sympathy for some of the great sweeps of twentieth-century determinist philosophy that deny the true freedom we have in Christ. The economic determinism of Marx reduced all endeavors to a prescribed set of inescapable economic responses. Once these economic forces were unleashed, the individual stood powerless—with no choice. Similarly, Freud and his successors would have us locked into sexual compulsions from which we cannot escape. There is no choice here either.

The truth is that Jesus is the Liberator. In freeing us, he also gives us the tools to use our freedom well. But there are many times when we want to discern the specific will of God for our lives, or when we are desperate for God's help to choose between two options, or when we are looking for God's green light in a challenging situation. And while God will not force us down a certain track—he wants us to make choices—he also wants to guide us, to give us advice. He knows us better than we know ourselves, he knows what is best for us, and he knows what choices will best lead us into the places to which he has called us.

CHOOSING WELL

Over the years I have found five simple steps that have helped me enormously in making difficult choices. Every step is taken in the light of the Holy Spirit guiding, leading, and prompting us. It is in the power of the life and teaching and example of Jesus that we can make these judgments.

1. CONSIDER

The first step in facing a major choice is to consider and weigh the range of options that are available, forming what I call early impressions.

Perhaps out of the blue, someone approaches you about a new business venture. What do you do? Is this a prompting from the Holy Spirit? It may well be, or it may not. At times like this, it's worth taking a leaf out of Mary's book: "But Mary treasured up all these things and pondered them in her heart" (Luke 2:19). Or we can be inspired by Joseph's father in Genesis 37: "Joseph's brothers envied him and were jealous of him, but his father observed the saying and pondered over it" (v. 11 AMP). *Treasured, observed,* and *pondered*—these words are wonderfully reassuring. The biblical precedent is that there is no need to rush; there is time to think, to weigh things, and to ask for discernment and wisdom. Saint Augustine took this point one step further, believing that the heart is something more than a place or feeling; it deals with one's proper identity in God. And therefore when we spend time listening to our consciences, the "silent clamor of the heart,"[1] we are likely to find God's truest call on our lives.

Perhaps a sense of restlessness has come upon you, and you wonder whether God is encouraging you to change jobs or move on to new pastures. It can be tempting in such moments to rush headlong into big decisions. But God often calls us to remain where we are and seek wisdom first. In 1 Corinthians, Paul encouraged his readers to "remain in the situation they were in when God called them" (1 Corinthians 7:20). The call of God does not necessitate radical changes to our work. What we first think is God prompting us to change jobs completely might actually be him encouraging us to take on new roles within our existing organizations, or simply to be better witnesses to our colleagues.

During times of restlessness, when we question whether or not a change is from God, it is useful to do some detailed research on what the options might be. Leaving one place without having any clear calling toward another is a difficult path to take, and unless you have been put in a situation where there is fraud, corruption, exploitation, or harassment that is compromising you, it is not a path I would recommend.

I have a friend named Harry who has recently made a bold and risky decision. He worked for a company whose ethics were questionable. After three years in the company, there came a time when Harry was asked to lie and to conceal some fraudulent dealings that were deceiving the client. Harry felt extremely uncomfortable about the way in which his senior management was behaving and felt he must resign. With a family to support and a mortgage to pay, and with no certain prospects of what was to come next, he made a brave call. He decided to pray about it for seven days, study the book of Proverbs to find wisdom, seek the counsel of some godly friends and his mentor, and hope that after a week the Lord would make it absolutely clear what he should do. Indeed, a week later he wrote his resignation letter, and a month later, he was on his own.

I remember talking to Harry in the wake of his resignation. It was a heavy weight he carried, but he knew that he couldn't continue working for a boss whose principles and working practices were so out of kilter with his own. He had always wanted to set up his own business, and in many ways, this felt like the opportunity to begin. I admired him for his integrity and I believe that God will honor him, through the new business, for the stand he has taken.

Such discernment comes only with wisdom. And wisdom comes only from spending time with God. We cannot work out the future on our own. As Paul wrote in 1 Corinthians, "'What no eye has seen, what no ear has heard, and what no human mind has conceived'— the things God has prepared for those who love him—these are the things God has revealed to us by his Spirit" (1 Corinthians 2:9–10).

People in all cultures desire wisdom. I think of elders in African communities who give sage advice reflecting the accumulation of good practices handed down from ancestors and distilled by them through observation and judgments. There is a buy-in by the tribe. They know, as we do, that mere knowledge is not the same as wisdom. But wisdom in these human settings, while separate from and superior to knowledge, is no more than pragmatism and experience elevated to a higher philosophical plane.

Wisdom in the Bible is of a different order. As the psalmist wrote, "The fool says in his heart, 'There is no God'" (Psalm 14:1). Those seeking wisdom seek God. They seek to live smartly in obedience to their callings. The book of Proverbs is a distillation of key practical concepts for wise living under God.

Eugene Peterson's *The Message* translation of the introduction to the book of Proverbs gives a brilliantly lucid summary:

> These are the wise sayings of Solomon,
> David's son, Israel's king—
> Written down so we'll know how to live well and right,
> to understand what life means and where it's going;
> A manual for living,
> for learning what's right and just and fair;
> To teach the inexperienced the ropes
> and give our young people a grasp on reality.
> There's something here also for seasoned men and women,
> still a thing or two for the experienced to learn—
> Fresh wisdom to probe and penetrate,
> the rhymes and reasons of wise men and women.
> (Proverbs 1:1–6 THE MESSAGE)

Wisdom is learning to discern God's ways in a cluttered world of opinions, personal thoughts, mantras, and make-believe. Wisdom is raw and real. Listening to God as we make our choices is key. We need times of withdrawal from the frenzy of life to quiet our spirits and listen to his wisdom. No choices will ever be made well without gleaning that wisdom.

In these times of listening quietly to God, the decisions that we are wrestling with will either fall away or grow in preeminence.

The stage of considering may also include reading about the subject. A friend of mine felt a certain prompting to work in Malaysia. It felt strange at first, as he hardly knew the country, but he took the idea seriously and started reading about the country's history, culture, and economic and social conditions. This research helped him think through what might or might not have been a nudge from God. As it happened, it all came together as he began to build a picture of a country he felt increasingly drawn to.

The stage of considering and pondering is demanding, as we are likely to get carried away on flights of fantasy about what could be. While we must avoid delusions and unrealistic daydreams, creative thinking is an important part of evaluating the way ahead. We are called to be creative in the image of the Creator—and God inhabits and uses our imaginations.

2. CONSULT

Critical to making good decisions is taking good advice. Why? For the simple reason that we don't have a monopoly on the experience or the insight needed for the situations we face. Others have been down the path before. The Bible urges us to find wisdom through many counselors: "For lack of guidance a nation falls, but victory is won through many advisors" (Proverbs 11:14). This is not justification for a focus group to gauge which way the wind is blowing. We must seek advice from those whom we trust to think upon things with wisdom and integrity. After all, opinions are many, but wisdom is select.

There are various categories of people whose advice is worth seeking:

+ Those who share our faith or our values, whether or not they are experts in our fields—different perspectives can help! I find it useful to talk and pray with a friend who is a worship leader and knows absolutely nothing about finance. He can discern from his dispassionate standpoint. The key is that he is kingdom-minded and wants to see the kingdom grow through me. His values and motivations, crucially, resemble my own.

+ Those who love us. They know us well, can speak truthfully and without agenda, and want the best for us.

+ Those who have experience and therefore wisdom in the area under discussion. With a work decision, these are people in the same field with the necessary experience to understand the choices and pitfalls.

+ Those who are in spiritual authority: our church leaders or our mentors, or perhaps trained life coaches or counselors, who ask the right questions.

Typically, it will be less helpful to seek counsel from the following:

+ Those who tend to agree with us, defer to us, or are in some way beholden to us.

+ Those with an agenda—or for whom the outcome of our decisions will have a positive or negative effect.

+ Those who tend to compete with us.

+ Those whom we feel close to but whose values differ from our own.

In 1 Kings 12, the people of Israel came to King Rehoboam and asked him to reduce the hours of work every Israelite man was required to donate to capital projects. First, he took time to consider. Then, he called the elders together and asked them, "How would you advise me to answer these people?" (v. 6). They gave a brilliant reply: "If today you will be a servant to these people and serve them and give them a favorable answer, they will always be your servants" (v. 7).

King Rehoboam chose to seek the counsel from the elders: they had experience, and he therefore could trust their wisdom. Indeed, they provided not only a wise answer but a godly way of thinking. Being a servant was key to being a good king. But he rejected their advice.

Next, he turned to the friends who had grown up with him, and he asked the same question. The answer could not have been more different: "These people have said to you, 'Your father put a heavy yoke on us, but make our yoke lighter.' Now tell them, 'My little finger is thicker than my father's waist. My father laid on you a heavy yoke; I will make it even heavier. My father scourged you with whips; I will scourge you with scorpions'" (vv. 10–11). They were rude, offensive, and ungodly. And above all, they were out of touch with the people they despised. King Rehoboam followed their advice nonetheless, rejected the wisdom of the elders, and increased the demands on his citizens. The people rebelled, and the civil unrest that would eventually divide Israel and Judah escalated.

King Rehoboam made the mistake of listening to those with whom he shared a history, who did not have the necessary wisdom to advise him well. We must choose carefully whose advice we listen to.

Mentoring is a practice recent generations have neglected. It is a great gift that bridges the divide between old and young, between those who are experienced and those who are searching in life, and it helps us avoid unnecessary mistakes. Bringing together mentors and mentees is one of the great services a church can do. I find it hugely stimulating spending time with the people I mentor. Although they kindly claim to learn from my experience, I always learn as much or more from them.

Accountability is one of the ways in which you can grow and mature in faith, including in your day-to-day decisions. I strongly encourage you to have someone, or better yet several people, to whom you can be accountable and listen to advice within a safe and affirming group. These must be people who are prepared to speak their minds, are emotionally supportive, and are not mere debating partners. Their motivations should be to build you up and not to use your invitation to be truthful as license to go in with the knife. Truth should always be spoken in love (Ephesians 4:15), out of a deep desire to honor you and to help you. When truth comes out of other motives, look for it elsewhere. Control freaks abound, who, under the guise of good advice, really want to control your life and the decisions you make. Have nothing to do with them, however spiritual they may appear. It is right to have the humility to listen with an open mind to others, but then we must weigh their advice and lay it out before the Lord. If we feel uncomfortable, we should trust our instincts, discard the advice, and shy away. No one owns you except Jesus Christ.

There is a modern danger of "oversharing" that has grown out of a belief, over the last decade or so, that by unburdening our inner selves to others, we gain wholeness. There are clearly advantages to being humble and vulnerable with those whom we trust and whom we have chosen to be accountable to. But restraint and measured disclosure need to be part of the balance.

How do we deal with prophetic words that are sometimes spoken over us? Paul urged us to use all the Spirit's gifts in our churches, "especially prophecy" (1 Corinthians 14:1). Prophecy is part of the life of a dynamic church. But words received in this way are to be thoroughly evaluated, as John urged his readers to do: "test the spirits to see whether they are from God" (1 John 4:1).

I am grateful for the many words spoken into my life over the years. Some are not easy to hear. Some have been fulfilled; others wait their time. I find it helpful to check the character of the person offering the word and determine whether he or she has used this gift before or whether I am the guinea pig! The fact that someone is new to prophecy is not a total obstacle, but knowing the person's level of experience makes me more receptive to the message. Does the word build me up or drag me down? Heavy judgment belongs to God and will be used sparingly. Does it agree with or contradict Scripture? If the word relates to a major career choice, I am even more cautious. A word is not necessarily right just because it seems to come through some supernatural source. But if the word resonates in my spirit, I will always pray that the Lord will confirm it to me through another person. And then I pray for the circumstances that have been prophesied to come about. I combine others' counsel with my own consideration: I watch, ponder, listen, and talk it through with others. There is no need to rush ahead of God's purposes, so I accept that his timing is part of the journey.

I have an acquaintance, Martin, who on two separate occasions received prophetic words of knowledge from trusted friends, telling him that he would set up his own business. It was something that Martin had always wanted to do, but he was unsure of the context and how to extract himself from his current job. He prayed about these prophetic words, and after a while, he found that he was agitated at work and unable to commit and give wholeheartedly to his job because of these prophecies hovering over him. He felt as if he were being disobedient to God for not setting up his own business. But then he heard a well-known prophet say there is often no specific timing to prophetic words. If the prophetic word to set up his own business was right, it could take place in six days, in six months, or in six years. This gave Martin relief and peace and the confidence to commit again to his current job, trusting that if these prophecies were from God, the opportunity to set up on his own would present itself at the right time.

3. CLARIFY

The apostle Paul exhorted the church in Thessalonica to *clarify* the callings of the Spirit. "Do not quench the Spirit," he said. "Do not treat prophecies with contempt, but test them all; hold on to what is good" (1 Thessalonians 5:19–21). It's sometimes easy to think that a sense of God's calling absolves us of the use of our critical faculties. But once we have considered and consulted, we need to take the time to clarify—to engage our reason—so that we might reflect on what we think has been revealed. This is the time to sift through all the information, using our analytical skills and our own self-understanding. For me, the best way of doing this is to make a list of pros and cons.

A colleague of mine was contemplating moving jobs. In order to help him clarify his options he created a PowerPoint presentation for himself, complete with appendices. Perhaps a little over the top, but it helped him clarify his thoughts.

On the other hand, a woman once asked me for advice on whether she should move jobs. It was a question she had posed, analyzed, assessed, and reassessed endlessly in her mind, until she was stuck in a circle of paralysis. I suggested that she try to reduce the issue to 140 characters and tweet it to me. This discipline toward greater clarity helped break the paralysis—and a decision was made.

At this point in the process of making a decision, we are hoping for some kind of breakthrough. In the book of Numbers, God spoke to Moses "intimately, in person, in plain talk without riddles" (Numbers 12:8 THE MESSAGE). That was an unusual experience, and there have been many occasions when I so long to hear God speak to me "intimately" and "in plain talk." But now, by his Spirit, he still speaks to all of us, though not usually audibly.

The conviction of the Spirit may take the form of an "aha" moment, a sense of a green light: a moment when suddenly, often effortlessly, the fog of the merry-go-round of thoughts just lifts. It happened to Peter when he was asked who Jesus was. It came to him with clarity in a single moment, but it followed a long time of walking the streets with Jesus, listening to his teaching, seeing his behavior in private as well as in public. And, in the "aha" moment, he declared, "You are the Christ, the Son of the living God" (Matthew 16:16 ESV).

We may, conversely, experience a red light. I remember when my wife, Fi, and I tried to purchase a very attractive property. All seemed well. We went through to the final stages of negotiation. We had viewed the property, seen its potential, and looked forward to the project of doing it up. We had considered all the angles: financial, personal, and practical. And yet as we prayed about it, we couldn't shake a nagging doubt that we might have been dragged along by the momentum of the deal.

One morning I woke up early and decided to write down the pros and cons for buying the house. I prayed over each one. Through this process, the right outcome became clearer and clearer, until the decision virtually made itself, by which I mean that the praying and pondering made a definitive result possible. It became clear to me that I had made a mistake: I had romanticized the idyllic countryside opportunities for recreation and enjoyment and had not done enough objective analysis to stop myself from being carried away. Attractive as the property undoubtedly was, I realized it would be a distraction from our primary calling.

After a conversation with Fi, I picked up the telephone to call our agent and explained that we would be withdrawing. He was understanding and helpful on how to extract us from a difficult situation. Somehow the prayers had also spilled over to the extraction process! Fi and I both felt enormous relief and never looked back.

But as I write this, I can remember the desk where I wrote the pros and cons. Above all, I remember the clarity of the decision. It was as if the con side of the page stood out highlighted, as the pro side faded away. Often at these times the Holy Spirit is like a bright LED light illuminating the key points on the tablet while the others fade into the background.

Fi and I were in agreement on this occasion, but sometimes clarity is provided by a couple's inability to unite around a decision. In such cases, we need to be honest with each other and work it through together, however hard the circumstances may be.

One of the greatest dangers in trying to make effective decisions is to be drawn too deeply into a process before you are ready. Extraction is much more difficult the farther along the path we travel.

Tom and Alison had to face the momentous decision of whether to move to Bogotá, Colombia. Tom had been offered a job with a company based there for a two- or three-year stint. He had been to several interviews, each one registering his intent that if he were to be offered the job, he and his wife would be ready to make the leap. However, it wasn't until the job offer came along that Alison suddenly had overwhelming fear about the prospect of relocating to such a foreign part of the world. It was as much a case of miscommunication between the two of them as anything else. Tom assumed that, as he went from each interview stage to the next, Alison was on board with the obvious outcome of events. She wrestled and wrestled with it, writing down all of her fears and praying over each one. Tom was desperate to accept the offer, but she couldn't bring herself to agree. They were keen to start a family, and the thought of raising small children in a dangerous part of South America was too daunting for her. To this day, they do not know if the decision they made was counter to God's will or was being led by God's will, but the outcome was that Tom got another job, happily, and life in London continued. Interestingly, though, God used the decision-making process to work on their marriage. The decision to withdraw was hard for Tom, and he had to learn to forgive Alison's reluctance to go to Bogotá, just as she had to forgive his reluctance to see and accept her fears. They both learned a lot about submitting to each other, about compromise, and about extending grace to each other. All these lessons have enriched and deepened their marriage.

The most important aspect of the clarifying process, however, is that we remain open to hearing from the Lord. When the prophet Samuel was called as a young boy in 1 Samuel 3, he assumed at first that he was being spoken to by his master, Eli. Every time God spoke, Samuel would get out of bed to find out what Eli wanted from him. It was only when he responded directly to God—"Speak, for your servant is listening" (v. 10)—that Samuel was ready to hear the message God had been trying to tell him.

We, like Samuel, need to invite God to speak into our lives. "Make me to know your ways, O LORD; teach me your paths" (Psalm 25:4 ESV) is a great verse to repeat when in the clarifying part of the decision making.

4. COURAGE

"Wait for the LORD; be strong and take heart and wait for the LORD" (Psalm 27:14).

It takes time to clarify decisions, especially major ones. We become impatient with God when decisions don't happen quickly. He often restrains us from moving forward, to test us or prevent us from charging headlong into a dead end. A nudge from God is what we need to know when the time of holding back is over.

The time of waiting is often plagued by doubt. In Shakespeare's *Troilus and Cressida*, the Trojan prince Hector said to his father, the king of Troy, "Modest doubt is called the beacon of the wise."[2]

Doubt will be with us in every one of our choices until we have made up our minds to walk a particular path—and sometimes afterward too. Doubt is the traveling companion of wisdom, and God can use our uncertainty as the humility necessary to remain dependent on him. Doubt is part of being human.

The Bible is full of wise people with doubts: Moses was unsure of his gifting to tackle Pharaoh; the Psalms are filled with David's doubts about himself, God, and those around him; Thomas doubted the resurrected Jesus; and the devil used doubt to try to thwart the start of Jesus' ministry, declaring, "If you are the Son of God . . ." (Matthew 4:6) and seeming to plant doubt in Jesus' mind about his very identity. Modest doubt—such a truth!

We need to live *through* doubt, not just *with* doubt, and that takes courage. Often decision making is tumultuous, like being tossed every way by the waves of the sea. At a crucial moment in my life, when I faced a period of insecurity about the future, I read Psalm 107:

> Some sailed over the ocean in ships,
>> earning their living on the seas.
> They saw what the LORD can do,
>> his wonderful acts on the seas.
> He commanded, and a mighty wind began to blow
>> and stirred up the waves.
> The ships were lifted high in the air
>> and plunged down into the depths.
> In such danger the sailors lost their courage;
>> they stumbled and staggered like drunks—
>> all their skill was useless.
> Then in their trouble they called to the LORD,
>> and he saved them from their distress.
> He calmed the raging storm,
>> and the waves became quiet.
> They were glad because of the calm,
>> and he brought them safe to the port they wanted.
> (vv. 23–30 GNT)

It was a brilliant and releasing picture. I felt the roller-coaster ride. And I felt the nausea of seasickness as I rode high in expectation, only to be rolled over by a crashing wave of dashed hope. It is true that when life feels turbulent, we often feel as if we are stumbling and staggering and losing our courage. This is a feeling I recognize during troubled times.

I have made no major decision in my life without finding myself crying out to God. And at times it has been from the depths of my being, as the psalmist described. But God brings the sailors and me out of distress. In the metaphorical stormy seas, the ships are piloted to safety, and so we are led through the turbulence into the right port. Now that is a liberating thought: after the terror of the ride, we are led to peaceful waters.

Making a final decision takes a deep breath and conviction. The Bible promises that if we are courageous in pursuing the ways of God, he stays with us. Undergirding all our decisions is this great reassurance: "The eternal God is your refuge, and underneath are the everlasting arms" (Deuteronomy 33:27).

5. Contented

Paul said in his letter to the Philippians that he had "learned to be content whatever the circumstances" (Philippians 4:11). This is about as difficult a lesson to learn as any. I am helped by the fact that he said "I have learned." Even for Paul, this response did not come instantly or effortlessly; it took application for him to be content regardless of outcome or circumstance. It's so easy to be content when we get what we want, not so easy when we don't.

A well-made decision results in experiencing relief that the decision has been made, as well as the "peace of God, which surpasses all understanding" (v. 7 ESV) that comes from the Lord. It is almost like a reward for the mental anguish that the decision-making process often entails, a kind of "well done, good and faithful servant" (Matthew 25:21).

Sometimes at this stage a confirmatory sign will corroborate the decision. Or looking back over past decisions can confirm a choice we have made was the right one. What we mustn't do, however, is live in the past. We mustn't look back and think, *If only this had happened*, or, *If only I'd not done that.*

Ecclesiastes tells us, "Do not say, 'Why were the old days better than these?'" (Ecclesiastes 7:10). This is a great piece of advice. It can be so easy to question our past decisions or wish that things had worked out differently. But this is fruitless. We can't even begin to imagine how God has used some of our strange decisions to shape us for the better.

Steve Jobs, the genius behind Apple, reflected that "you can't connect the dots looking forward; you can only connect them looking backward."[3] He had dropped out of college but kept returning to attend the classes he found interesting. The one that particularly made an impression was the class on calligraphy.

He said, "I learned about serif and sans serif typefaces, about varying the amount of space between different letter combinations, about what makes great typography great. It was beautiful, historical, artistically subtle in a way that science can't capture, and I found it fascinating."[4]

None of this had any practical application to his life at that time. However, ten years later, when he was designing the first Macintosh computer, it all came back to him. And he designed it all into the Mac. It was the first computer with beautiful typography. If he had never dropped in on that single college course, the Mac would not have had multiple typefaces or proportionally spaced fonts.

He said, "Of course it was impossible to connect the dots looking forward when I was in college. But it was very, very clear looking backward 10 years later."[5] And so it is with our lives.

We need to cultivate a relationship of trust with the Father, who loves us. He will guide us by his Holy Spirit to make the next choice the best choice.

It can be dangerous to seek confirmation of your choice by analyzing whether you now have the perfect job or the perfect life.

Nothing is perfect this side of heaven, and often God allows us to choose pathways that will be filled with challenges and obstacles. These do not mean that we have taken the wrong path.

There are clearly times when we make decisions we regret. If I make a mistake, I am always comforted by knowing that I took care in the process: I considered thoughtfully, I sought the counsel of others, I took steps to clarify—and I chose the best available option at the time in the light of the information and alternatives available. We cannot see into the future, so I try not to beat myself up for decisions that don't end up as I had hoped. I do my best not to linger or indulge in introspective self-examination. Of course, sometimes, in retrospect, I see that I acted in haste, or at a time of distress, or without taking time to hear God's voice. What then? Does it mean that I am forever trapped in a wrong path? No. That is when I realize that God's grace is sufficient (2 Corinthians 12:9). If I have done something wrong, then I may need to repent, set the record straight, and allow God to lead me without having to undo the decisions.

When I was young, I had a long-held dream to go to Oxford University. I was obsessed with the notion of it. And then I received a rejection letter. There was no place for me there. I was absolutely devastated as a dream fizzled out in front of me.

Then, out of the blue and quite unexpectedly, I got an offer from Cambridge University. I know you might well think, *What a spoiled brat to have had such a choice, to have to put up with Cambridge!* But disappointment is not rational but emotional—and I felt acute disappointment over the lost dream of Oxford. However, I went to Cambridge University. As I was a late applicant, there was no place for me to stay in the college, and I had to live five miles outside the university. When I first arrived, I had no friends and I was miserable.

But, as a result of being there, my faith in Jesus Christ came alive because of some of the friends I did eventually make. God used a great disappointment to grow me and nurture me in incredible ways. It was there that I met Nicky Gumbel, the founder of Alpha, and Nicky Lee, the founder of the Marriage Course, who remain two of my closest friends to this day. I made more friends than I could ever have imagined in that place, and we began to see God working in our lives and in the lives of other people around us. My dream to go to Oxford might have fizzled and died. But God's dream for me was just beginning.

CALLED TO THE CROSSROADS

The fact that God gives us choices is an incredible, liberating truth. But it can also be a scary one. It means that we will eventually be held accountable for those choices. Our work will be tested: "the fire will test the quality of each person's work" (1 Corinthians 3:13). This is a sobering thought. What we build and, more particularly, *how* we build, has eternal consequences. My business, if built on good values with Christ as the foundation, will survive any testing by fire. Conversely, if I build a business by deceiving or exploiting others, by choosing to act in underhanded ways or by breaking the law or by failing to operate with transparency and decency, then my work will not withstand the judgment test of 1 Corinthians 3:13. Nor will it give me the peace within which to enjoy the fruit of my labors.

But it's not simply by our ethical choices that we will be judged. We will also be asked to account for the choices we didn't make— moments when we let the status quo linger because it was simply too difficult to confront those nagging questions that lingered in the recesses of our minds.

In Saint Paul's letter to the Ephesians, he begged them to "live a life [literally "walk in the path"] *worthy* of the calling you have received" (Ephesians 4:1, emphasis added). Paul was urging his congregation to make choices worthy of the calling that God had placed on their lives, not choices dictated by the immediate pressures of the moment. He was urging them to be intentional in their decision making and not to resign themselves to going through the motions. *The Message* version of Ephesians 4 translates as follows:

> In light of all this, here's what I want you to do. While I'm locked up here, a prisoner for the Master, I want you to get out there and walk—better yet, run!—on the road God called you to travel. I don't want any of you sitting around on your hands. I don't want anyone strolling off, down some path that goes nowhere. And mark that you do this with humility and discipline—not in fits and starts, but steadily, pouring yourselves out for each other in acts of love, alert at noticing differences and quick at mending fences. (vv. 1–3)

This is important to remember when we come to what I call *crossroads moments*. Sometimes I have prayed with people and felt clearly that God was bringing them to a crossroads. New opportunities were opening up or circumstances were changing, and God was forcing them into making choices about what their lives were going to look like going forward.

I think of Tim, a successful banker in London who was caught up in the banking crisis. He was exhausted and felt, in my view rightly, that it was time to leave. Eventually, his exhaustion brought him to a crossroads moment, where he had to think about what might be next. It wasn't easy or simple, but then life-changing decisions often aren't.

When we come to such points, the pressure to make a decision can be unbearable. Confusion reigns, and the intensity of frustrated praying merely exacerbates an already-difficult situation. I sympathize with those in this position. I have confronted many crossroads threatening to detract from the very relationship of trust that is needed to navigate the way ahead.

Yet, without a shadow of doubt, I believe that God allows these crossroads to come into our lives in order to build up our trust in him and to strengthen us for the road he has called us down. Very often, a choice is complicated by alternative options. In my experience—painful as it is to have to examine the crossroads—it is in these moments that we truly confront the questions of our callings and our relationships with Christ. His purpose is always to bring glory to his name, and we are called to make our crossroads choice in the light of that fact. As we take our first faltering steps in a new direction, God promises that he will be beside us, supporting us. But the choice has to be ours.

The provocative, and yet reassuring, promise from Jeremiah says: "This is what the LORD says: 'Stand at the crossroads and look; ask for the ancient paths, ask where the good way is, and walk in it, and you will find rest for your souls'" (Jeremiah 6:16).

No person who seriously wishes to make the most of his or her life will escape crossroads moments. It is in these moments that we trust that what appears to be an ending is, in fact, part of Christ's plan, and that it also contains a beginning and a new path. The end of one stage of life is not the end of the calling. God has not finished with us. After all, when Jesus cried out on the cross, "It is finished" (John 19:30), he did not say that he was done. He rose again. A task had been completed, but he wasn't finished. He could now start a resurrected life.

Some years ago I talked to a friend who was a brilliant executive in one of the major oil companies operating in London. He was at a crossroads in his life: Should he leave his firm and instead seek ordination to the priesthood? It would be hard to explain the choice to his colleagues and peers rationally or in language that they would understand. He knew this. But above all he sensed a new direction to his life, prompted by the Spirit of God. He followed that path, hesitatingly at first, but then he saw the conviction grow. He left the oil business and began training for ordination. A new path, a new direction, and a fresh word of God changed the course of his career.

Now, many years later, Justin Welby is the archbishop of Canterbury and leader of the worldwide Anglican Communion. As I sat with my wife in Canterbury Cathedral and watched him being installed as the new archbishop, I thought back to those conversations. I was deeply moved as I remembered God's promise in Isaiah: "I make known the end from the beginning" (Isaiah 46:10).

KEEPING THE FLAME ALIVE

All of us find times when we question the choices we have made and doubt the direction of our lives. When we have made decisions about our careers and are perhaps two or three years into these roles, how do we keep the flame alive? How do we ensure that we do not become complacent, lazy, or apathetic about our callings?

- **INVEST IN OURSELVES.** It is important to invest in ourselves and in our callings. A calling is not just a kickoff but a continuous process of investing in our lives. We need to be watchful of our characters; we must examine our reactions to people and situations. Character matters more than any success at work. I find that reading a biography of someone who has faced problems and overcome them can be an inspiring way to keep on my toes at work. Taking a course on leadership development would be a positive way to stay focused on equipping for future challenges and ensuring we are keeping fresh, new perspectives on our work.
- **KNOW HIS WAYS.** Seeking out God's ways in our lives is a daily activity. We cannot let our hearts go astray. Psalm 95 puts it very clearly: "For forty years I was angry with that generation; I said, 'They are a people whose hearts go astray, and they have not known my ways'" (v. 10).
- **STAY HUMBLE.** This is key to refreshing our callings. When we lay down our agendas at the foot of the cross and humble

ourselves, we are reminded of who we are in Christ. As the psalmist said, "He guides the humble in what is right and teaches them his way" (Psalm 25:9). It is an essential requirement for keeping the flame alive that we renew our dependence on him each day. He is the keeper of the flame and the one who renews all things.

+ **CONFESS ANYTHING DISPLEASING TO GOD.** In this way we keep the flame open rather than suffocating it under wraps for fear of what might be exposed. "You, Lord, are forgiving and good, abounding in love to all who call to you" (Psalm 86:5).

+ **CLAIM AN UNDIVIDED HEART.** Nothing douses the flame of the Spirit as rapidly as a divided allegiance, when we mix our callings with our competitive or selfish agendas. "Teach me your way, LORD, that I may rely on your faithfulness; give me an undivided heart, that I may fear your name" (v. 11). If I am ever asked to make a choice of whom I would follow to work, or whom I would want to emulate, it would always be those who have big, generous, and undivided hearts.

If you stay strong and humble by serving others, worshipping God, and being strong in the Word and watchful of your character, you will remain fully alive in your calling. As the writer of Deuteronomy so vividly implores us, we have a choice between "life and death, blessings and curses. Now choose life" (Deuteronomy 30:19). After all, the choice will last forever!

———— SIX ————

CALLED TO COURAGE

EVEN IF A DECISION SEEMS EASY OR THE WAY AHEAD SEEMS clear, barriers can stop us from stepping into the callings God has placed on our lives. What holds us back? Apathy can leave us struggling to see his paths. Selfish desires can lead us in the opposite direction of that which God intends for us. Distractions can divert our attentions. Greed can cloud our judgments. Above all, however, *fear* can hold us back from the callings God has for us.

I know from my own experiences, and those of countless others, that fear and anxiety are apt to stalk us. Fear can come in many forms—it might be fear of personal harm, or fear of emotional distress, or fear of financial hardship. Depending on what we feel we are being called into, all sorts of fears might arise.

In this chapter, I want to focus on one particular type of fear. It's a fear that nobody is exempt from—a fear that can cripple us even when we have our priorities correctly aligned and are wholeheartedly committed to following God's call. This is the fear of failure. I believe this fear constitutes the greatest barrier to our callings.

But what fear bricks up, grace breaks up. Overcome the fear of failure, and we allow God's favor to flood in and transform the future. God's favor is the love that the Father naturally wants to show to his children. Parents want the best for their children, longing to find opportunities to encourage and inspire them. That is certainly my wish as a father for my own children. How much more, then, does God, our Father, want to encourage and inspire us? How much more does he long to break the paralysis of fear and anxiety in our lives?

Fear of failure is born of ignorance and uncertainty: ignorance of events that will shape the future, and uncertainty as to how we will react to them. In many ways, this is perfectly natural. We can't control the future. We don't know what is around the corner. Life, as we know from Forrest Gump's mother, is "like a box of chocolates—you never know what you're gonna get."[1]

I cannot break through the brick wall of fear that so often stands in the way of the next move of God in my life. *But God can.*

Disappointments can drain us of energy and fill us with doubt about our own abilities and judgments. Failures can sometimes bring us to a grinding halt for fear of anything so crushing, so humiliating, or so hopeless ever happening again. Anxiety is exhausting because we spend a huge amount of time and energy worrying about events that usually never happen. Most of the time our worst-case scenarios don't come to fruition, yet we rehearse them as if they are realities. A friend of mine regularly reminds me, "Deal with what you know."

Jesus concurs! In the Sermon on the Mount, Jesus made it clear that we are foolish to fret about the future over which we have no control: "Therefore do not worry about tomorrow, for tomorrow will worry about itself. Each day has enough trouble of its own" (Matthew 6:34). It's a call to all of us to live in the moment and for the day. This is not intended to make us ditch all future plans but to choose not to worry about all the angst-inducing issues that (possibly) lie ahead of us.

So how do we fight anxiety and fear? How do we deal with disappointment and dashed hopes? How do we overcome these obstacles that so often slow us down and prevent us from walking confidently into our God-given callings?

There is a passage in Exodus 15 that has radically changed my perspective on dealing with the inevitable disappointments in life. This is the chapter that records the extraordinary circumstances in which Moses led the people of Israel out of Egypt. They had this wonderful dream that one day they would live in the land of milk and honey, in the land of Canaan, away from the Egyptian slave drivers. And sure enough, one of the greatest miracles of all time occurred when the Red Sea was parted and they could pass through, unscathed and free.

Yet only three days later, they started grumbling: "When they came to Marah, they could not drink its water, because it was bitter. . . . So the people grumbled against Moses, saying, 'What are we to drink?'" (vv. 23–24). Disappointment comes quickly.

Three days earlier, the Israelites had seen God save them in the most incredible of circumstances. Is the Lord who could separate the Red Sea not the one who could also give them water to drink? But they started complaining and grumbling, much the same way we do. We have great expectations of God, and suddenly something happens and we become dogged by disappointment.

"Moses cried out to the LORD, and the LORD showed him a piece of wood. He threw it into the water, and the water became fit to drink" (v. 25). (God was, of course, perfectly able to change the water without human intervention, but he chose to use Moses, drawing him into the miracle and demonstrating his involvement. We work with him, and he works through us.) The episode concludes: "For I am the LORD, who heals you" (v. 26). When translated literally, God actually said, "I am Jehovah-Rapha"—the word *Rapha* means "I am the one who takes the bitter, and makes it sweet."

Disappointments can be overwhelming: disappointment in ourselves for the mistakes we've made or the grades we failed to achieve, or disappointment in others or in circumstances that have not turned out well. These past disappointments and failures can be crippling—they hold us back, making us think twice about trusting God or taking a risk in faith.

The key to overcoming such fear is recognizing we have a God who is bigger than even our greatest failings. How often have I tasted the bitterness of disappointments, fears, and failures, only to find that, by his Spirit, sweetness arises out of them? Years after a bitter disappointment, I realize that the very failure has taught me lessons I would never have learned otherwise, and that the result was far more enriching than success at the time could ever have been.

Quite recently, I had to face the pain of acute disappointment and failure. About two years ago, a number of colleagues and I began to create a private investment fund. We rented offices; we recruited people to work on this new idea; we started raising money. Then, a few months into the new venture, it was quite clear that the market had moved against us, and we had to face a decision of whether to linger on or to cut our losses and admit failure—not an experience I'd often had before. But there it was—the heartache, the failed dreams, the unmet expectations, the disappointment of having to let people go. Still lingering was belief that it might have been able to work, if only we'd had more time and the markets had been a little more moderate. But it was the end of the road. It was hard trying to dodge the inevitable questions about how things were shaping up in the new venture. The failure was acute and the pain intense. It still is.

But I take my strength in the knowledge that Jehovah-Rapha, my God and my Savior who turns the bitter into the sweet, will take my struggle and work on me in the midst of this failure.

LEARNING TO FAIL

Failure is best faced squarely in the eye. So often we strive to make sure that, at all costs, we avoid the pain of failure—but God is larger than the biggest failure in your life. He redeems, transforms, and turns what is bitter into something sweet.

J. K. Rowling, author of the Harry Potter novels, once said, "It is impossible to live without failing at something, unless you live so cautiously that you might as well not have lived at all—in which case, you fail by default."[2]

She went on to say,

> Ultimately, we all have to decide for ourselves what constitutes failure, but the world is quite eager to give you a set of criteria if you let it. So I think it fair to say that by any conventional measure, a mere seven years after my graduation day, I had failed on an epic scale. An exceptionally short-lived marriage had imploded, and I was jobless, a lone parent, and as poor as it is possible to be in modern Britain, without being homeless. The fears that my parents had had for me, and that I had had for myself, had both come to pass, and by every usual standard, I was the biggest failure I knew. . . .
>
> I was set free because my greatest fear had been realised and I was still alive, and I still had a daughter whom I adored, and I had an old typewriter and a big idea. And so rock bottom became the solid foundation on which I rebuilt my life.[3]

A typewriter and a big idea—out of which came Harry Potter. That was all J. K. Rowling needed. We just need those ideas that lie dormant within us to be awakened. We just need the courage to let those ideas and dreams, the callings God has placed on our lives, grow into reality whatever the circumstances.

Doubtless, we will all fail at something at some point in our lives. But we will never *be* failures. For that to happen Christ within us would have to fail. And he won't. It's a vital distinction. When we do not grasp this, we can easily spiral downward. What makes it so difficult is when we feel as if we keep on failing. Thomas Edison, faced with this frustration, asserted that he had not failed. Instead, he said, "I know several thousand ways that won't work!"[4]

There's a lesson for us here. Don't linger on the inevitable failures. Do learn, but don't look back, and certainly not in anger. Move on in confidence that you have God by your side.

One hears many leaders and managers declaring in a blustering tone to their teams, "Failure is not an option!" But this is wrong. Being willing to fail is an essential part of our callings.

As Christians, we are carriers of a great hope: hope in a God who is above and beyond all things, hope that places of darkness and despair might be transformed into places of life and light. But the hardest thing about this great hope is that we don't know how it is going to play out in our individual lives. We are called to face an uncertain future in confidence, but we are not fortune-tellers. Ecclesiastes 8:7 says, "Since no one knows the future, who can tell someone else what is to come?" It is only God who sees all things and knows all things.

Whenever we step out in faith, we take a risk. Whenever we dare to hope in the face of hopelessness or dream the impossible dream, whenever we are willing to try what the world might dismiss as foolish, we are not doing any of these things in absolute assurance that our attempts will succeed. Even risks taken in the power of God are still risks! God is not an on-demand enabler who makes our every endeavor succeed. Every dreamer and schemer of the kingdom knows deep disappointment. Part of Christian faith, part of being willing to dream, means being willing to fail. It means being willing to take risks for God, in the knowledge that God is in control and we are not.

This is easy to say on paper, but in practice it can be a hard and painful lesson to learn. And once we have been burned from one risk, it can be incredibly difficult to take another. Fear of failure can stop us in our tracks. But if we're not taking risks, then we are not living a life of faith, and "without faith it is impossible to please God" (Hebrews 11:6). Playing safe is no answer to the fear of failure; it will never satisfy.

In the parable of the talents, which we find in Matthew 25, the master rewarded the servants who were willing to risk failure to grow what they had been given. The one who played it safe, burying his treasure in the ground because he saw the master as a hard man—a ruthless bully who didn't tolerate failure—received the master's wrath. Those who trusted in the goodness of the master were rewarded.

What would the master have said to one of those servants if he had tried to invest the money wisely, but forces outside his control had robbed him of that with which he had been entrusted? Only a hypocrite would have punished such a faithful servant. No, a good master would have said exactly the same to the servant who had tried and failed as he did to the one who succeeded: "Well done, good and faithful servant. You have been faithful over a little; I will set you over much" (v. 23 ESV).

To those who have taken a risk in faith and found their hopes come crashing back to earth, to those who dared to dream that God might do a new thing but have been left crushed and disappointed, Jesus, too, says, "Well done, good and faithful servant!" Well done for dreaming, for being willing to see things as they might yet be rather than as they are. Well done for stepping out in faith despite your fear and your hesitancy. Well done for daring to think that hope might not be lost.

Our failures are not failures in the eyes of God. When we step out in faith, we always triumph, whether or not we are successful on our terms.

But Jesus is also able to take our failures and mold them into something new. Some years ago I was affected deeply by the plight of the debts that the developing world owed to the developed world. It seemed wrong that irresponsible bankers and governments from these impoverished countries should have borrowed so much. As these were some of the poorest countries, they were unable to repay the interest, let alone the capital that was owed. Sometimes the borrowing had been fueled by corruption and government greed. Every cent spent on paying off debt was a cent not spent on education and health care. These countries were trapped. To make matters worse, the debt was invariably in dollars or other hard currencies. They were unable to repay, with crippling consequences for the ordinary people who had to shoulder massive burdens for the repayment of interest.

A group of friends and Christian leaders got together to see whether we could do something. We developed an imaginative program called BONDFIRE, which would seek to raise public awareness of this problem and would print documents that looked like loan documents—and then have a massive bonfire to show solidarity for all initiatives aimed at getting lender nations to write off these debts.

I invested some money, enlisted economists to write articles, and asked theologians to give reasons why debt relief of this kind was not fueling irresponsible behavior but part of a Christian response to injustice. I confess I was rather pleased with the strong support I mustered. And yet the campaign failed. I felt this acutely. The need seemed so obvious.

There were a number of good reasons why the project failed, including our failure to persuade the public that this debt was different from an excessive personal credit card debt.

But what appeared at the time to be a failure subsequently succeeded, as several initiatives from other agencies built a better argument and had greater traction. Campaigns such as Jubilee 2000 and Make Poverty History, which enjoyed endorsements from celebrities including Bono, succeeded. Some of the most crippling debt was written off. There lay a great lesson for the decade ahead, one I have learned again and again. The most important thing is not that *my* project succeeds, but that good is done.

Who knows how Jesus might use our failures? Sometimes just the act of failing can help us forge a deeper connection with the world around us. When we dare to reveal the fact that we feel weak, confused, angry, and ashamed, it is then that others can connect with us because they know how to relate to us. In these moments, our common humanity is more effective than any religious talk. Our lives become authentic, affirming, and accessible. Even our moments of failure and disappointment can be how God prepares us for the way ahead.

Take the story of Joseph, found in the book of Genesis. Joseph was the favored son of his father, with dreams of power and glory, when his jealous brothers kidnapped him and sold him into slavery. Later, he became the committed and trusted servant of Potiphar, an official of the Egyptian pharaoh. But when Potiphar's wife falsely accused Joseph of assault, he was condemned to prison indefinitely.

At this point, Joseph must have considered his life a complete failure. He must have been utterly dejected. But it was from that dark and hopeless prison that God raised Joseph up to become the second most powerful man in all Egypt. There he learned the skills of leadership. It was through the experiences of his fellow prisoners that God showed him how to interpret dreams. And it was because of his relationships there that Joseph came to the attention of the pharaoh as someone who could explain nightmares.

Through Joseph's failures God prepared him to be the person he was called to be—the man who would save huge swaths of the Middle East from the ravages of famine.

This points to one great truth that I have continuously learned throughout my life: often the long and tortuous route is more fruitful than the quick shortcut. We frequently learn deeper lessons in the byways than on the highways.

Like Joseph, Nelson Mandela was someone who seemed to have utterly failed. Imprisoned for twenty-seven years, he must have thought, sitting in his cell on Robben Island, that he had reached a dead end. Unable to communicate with the outside world, he must have felt his struggle for freedom was a distant memory and no more. The future was bleak.

That cell was the most hidden of byways, but, ultimately, it was the path to his life calling. If he had not been locked up and brutalized through all those years, he would never have become the iconic leader not just of a nation but of the world. It was in those dark cells that he learned the painful truths of forgiveness and reconciliation, which he was able to put into practice once he was released. Because of that grueling experience, he understood forces of institutional evil that corrupted people into following a hideous ideology.

Mandela did not remain hidden. But many of us do. Unlike Mandela, we often do not see the extent of our own fruitfulness. There's a wonderful quote from Henri Nouwen that reads, "The beauty of life is that it bears fruit long after life itself has come to an end."[5]

We see the lasting effects of a fruitful life in the biblical story of Leah, Joseph's stepmother and Jacob's first wife. For many years, Jacob worked for his uncle Laban in order to gain the hand of Laban's beautiful daughter Rachel. After this period of work, however, Laban tricked Jacob into marrying Rachel's sister, Leah. From that point on, Leah pretty much remained in the shadows. She never knew the extent of her own fruitfulness. She was disliked, dishonored, disappointed, and always referred to in contrast to her sister's beauty. She was neither respected by her father nor loved by her husband, Jacob, who lusted after her sister. The only reason he slept with her for the first time was because he was inebriated after their wedding party.

But Leah's one gift, which distinguished her from her sister, was that she was fertile. After she gave birth to her first son, Reuben, she thought, "Now my husband will love me" (Genesis 29:32 ESV). After her second son, Simeon, and her third, Levi, she hoped desperately that her husband would be a companion to her (v. 34). But he was not. Then, she discovered a key that unlocked her life—and it will unlock yours. After having a fourth son, she said, "This time I will praise the LORD" (v. 35). Reuben, Simeon, and Levi would be fathers to three of the great tribes of Israel. But her fourth son, Judah, would be ancestor to David and ultimately Jesus! Leah learned the great truth that only God loves us unconditionally. She failed to win her husband's love, but submission to God in praise transformed her life.

As J. K. Rowling would ask, whose version of "failure" did Leah measure her life by? In the world's eyes, she had very little to offer. But God chose her as a mother to the ancient nation of Israel. Thousands of years later, the full effect was seen in the person of Jesus Christ.

At the point of his death, Jesus himself must have seemed like the ultimate failure. All those promises made at his birth. All those miraculous signs and wonders. All that incredible potential, yet here he was, nailed to a tree, breathing his last breath, just a few years into his ministry and well before his thirty-fifth birthday. Most of his followers had abandoned him, and there was no hope for the movement he had started. Except, of course, that his apparent failure was not the last word. With his resurrection and ascension, the greatest movement that has ever been was birthed, touching the lives of billions of people.

The death and resurrection of Jesus show just how powerless fear really is. With God, we don't know what's going to happen. We don't know how he might use our apparent failings for his glory and his works. In the resurrection of Christ even the great, final fear— fear of death—is rendered impotent.

FLIP THE FEAR

In the financial market, the Vix Index, also known as the "Fear Index," measures the fears of investors. When investors are concerned by future instability and uncertainty, the index goes up. This echoes the fear index in our own lives, which tends to oscillate, often quite sharply.

We need to be as vigilant in our own lives as a trader would be watching the impact of fear on the markets. As we become more fearful of the future, we need to be more active in taking necessary steps to protect ourselves from this fear. God is open 24/7 to swap our fears for favor. But we need to initiate that trade.

Here are five "fear flippers"—tools that will help us turn from fear to faith.

1. LOOK TO JESUS

Jesus encouraged his disciples, "In this world you will have trouble. But take heart! I have overcome the world" (John 16:33). He could not have been clearer. Fear is a powerful impostor, but Jesus has overcome the world that tries to breathe fear into life. And when we come to know in our hearts that we have secure life in Christ and that he loves us and guides us, the world changes. As the apostle John put it, "perfect love casts out fear" (1 John 4:18 ESV).

On the cross, Jesus made a spectacle of the powers of evil (Colossians 2:15); he literally disarmed the enemy. His cry from the cross—"It is finished!"—meant that his work of overcoming every resistance to God's rule was done. But more than that, through his resurrection, he conquered death. So now death, the ultimate enemy, can be taunted with the rhetorical question: "O death, where is your sting?" (1 Corinthians 15:55 ESV). It needs no answer. The same power that was at work when Jesus rose from the dead works in us, too (Ephesians 1:19–20), and no failure or fall can separate us from it. As Paul wrote so beautifully to the Romans:

> Who shall separate us from the love of Christ? Shall trouble or hardship or persecution or famine or nakedness or danger or sword? . . . No, in all these things we are more than conquerors through him who loved us. For I am convinced that neither death nor life, neither angels nor demons, neither the present nor the future, nor any powers, neither height nor depth, nor anything else in all creation, will

be able to separate us from the love of God that is in Christ Jesus our Lord. (Romans 8:35–39)

The God who has overcome all things is with us and beside us. Failure, suffering, pain, and trouble all might come. But our God is greater than anything on this earth. And "if God is for us, who can be against us?" (v. 31).

2. BREAK THE LIE

Behind almost every fear lurks a lie from our enemy, the father of lies (John 8:44). And contrary to what some people think, the devil is still spreading his deception. He is a fecund liar, fathering deception, despair, and discouragement.

There will always be a battle surrounding the Christian life. Fear is such an insurgent. It wants to rule without any responsibility; it wants to destabilize us wherever possible.

But the spirit of fear cannot form a bridgehead into the land occupied by a person whose trust is set on the Lord. The enemy can only sow trouble, anxiety, and depression; he cannot reap. That is the key to understanding fear. His only ability is to undermine our callings.

The most powerful understanding I have of this undermining role came to me during a time of real spiritual battle. The more I thought about the tricks of the evil one, the more I realized that he has one colossal failing: he is not God. He is not omniscient. He therefore cannot know—and will never know—the future. He will fight, but he cannot win; the battle has already been won by God.

The devil therefore needs to deceive us into believing that he knows and can govern our futures. He relies on us to do his work: the work of eroding our trust in Jesus Christ. He will throw out misinformation, falsehood, and anxiety in the hope of causing as much disruption as possible. He has no idea which of his lies will hit the mark, because he simply does not know what the Lord's plans are for our lives. He is therefore disarmed by the truth, which is Christ in us, and it is this truth that sets us free (v. 32).

Unless we feed fear, it will not grow to be powerful. Ultimately, it is illusory and without substance. Gripping and enthralling, yes, and at times utterly destructive, but it is a deception and has to pass. It has no energy of itself. Fear is parasitic, sucking life from us to sustain its claim on our lives.

Fear makes a powerful attempt to grip our attention. A knot in the pit of our stomachs reminds us of its physical consequences, as does the metallic taste of excess adrenaline in our mouths. But once we know that behind most fears lurks a lie, then we can ignore it by remembering God's truths in our lives.

3. SPEAK THE WORD

Scripture is a powerful weapon and has "divine power to demolish strongholds" (2 Corinthians 10:4). Words of God's love, of his faithful promises, and of his power—when spoken out in faith—can dismantle the gruesome blockades that fear tries to build around us. If I sense that my own fear index is rising, I vigorously reject the oncoming fears, sometimes quite loudly and always with the sword of the Spirit—which is the Word of God—wielded high above my head. I brandish "the one who is in [me] is greater than the one who is in the world" (1 John 4:4) as a sword of words. It cuts the enemy down to size!

My friend Charles used to work at a large US investment bank, where he had a boss who used fear to control his team. His boss was malevolent, micromanaging, and sarcastic, and the team was both terrified of him and debilitated by him. Charles suffered from terrible insomnia as a result and eventually had to leave the company due to the stress caused by this boss—though not before officially reporting him to the authorities within the organization.

He had worked for months in an atmosphere of fear and anxiety. It is the great myth of the workplace that instilling fear produces results. It is, of course, true that a boss whom you fear can get some assignments done through pressure and bullying. But it is not sustainable, nor is it moral.

Charles's colleagues also suffered the effects of this bully. But, two years later and now in a new career that he loves, he reflects on how God carried him through that testing period. Often, he told me, he would walk into the office speaking under his breath, "so do not fear, for I am with you; do not be dismayed, for I am your God. I will strengthen you and help you; I will uphold you with my righteous right hand" (Isaiah 41:10). He put Post-it notes on his computer with verses that would sustain him during the day. And so it was that Charles, though experiencing what felt like an inescapable nightmare, could still find hope in Paul's experience of being "hard pressed on every side, but not crushed; perplexed, but not in despair; persecuted, but not abandoned; struck down, but not destroyed" (2 Corinthians 4:8–9).

We have in Jesus the greatest teacher of all time. We would do well to learn from him. In the desert, the devil offered him a range of temptations: food (during a time of fasting), power (when Israel was ruled by Romans), and loyalty (from his adversary). Jesus met each temptation head-on with a sharp retort quoting Scripture. Jesus replied, "It is written, 'Man shall not live on bread alone.' . . . It is written, 'Worship the Lord your God and serve him only.' . . . It is said: 'Do not put the Lord your God to the test'" (Luke 4:4, 8, 12). There is no gap in the reply, no hesitation, and above all no need to add a measure of logical debate or conversation to empower the riposte. The Word doesn't need our assistance. It has momentum of its own.

When I was in the middle of a major transaction for the acquisition of a large London store, I sensed enormous angst that would not leave me. It was unsettling. I was unsure of what to do. I had to speak to one of the parties involved on the telephone and felt extremely anxious about the call. As I was waiting to be put through, the music playing on the phone was the theme from *Chariots of Fire*. As I listened, I had a prompting to look in the Bible. And there in 2 Kings 6 was the extraordinary assurance that there were unseen chariots of fire protecting Elisha from harm: "Then the Lord opened the servant's eyes, and he looked and saw the hills full of horses and chariots of fire all around Elisha" (v. 17). Speaking out that word in faith was a breakthrough and gave me great assurance.

4. Remember to trust

Fear cannot create. If teams of professionals need to find creative solutions to different issues, then they have to work in an atmosphere of mutual trust. Firstly they need to know that their boss trusts them—which, of course, leads them to trust in return. What follows is productive and fruitful collaboration. Fear can force employees to execute projects, but it cannot energize people. Fear is crippling and inhibiting, and it is one of the most dehumanizing forces in the workplace.

I recently read an inspiring article about the way in which Richard Branson runs one of his companies, Virgin.[6] His employees are free to leave the office at any particular time; they are not restricted to the 8:00 a.m. to 6:00 p.m. routine. The deal is that they fulfill their tasks to the best of their abilities and complete all their work to the standard that is expected of them. They can also take as much annual leave as they like, based on the same principle. In so doing, Branson is creating an atmosphere of total trust and freedom. It is a risky, bold strategy for Branson to take, but by all accounts it is paying off. The employees feel empowered and trusted; the result is that they do their best for Branson because they want to serve him and please him, not because they have to. This is the very opposite of Charles's experience in the bank.

At a human level, Branson's model reminds us that reciprocal trust builds flourishing relationships, and flourishing relationships build successful organizations.

At a divine level, God's ultimate act of trust is to give each of us free will, which empowers us to trust God in return. When we remember that we are trusted, we are emboldened to stand against the claim that fear has the power to dominate our lives. By the Spirit of God, we can consciously embrace the truth we know about God's character. We choose to walk not by fear but by trust—by faith.

5. THROW YOURSELF IN

In times of intense pressure and equally intense fear, we must use all these strategies. In my experience, fear cannot be dealt with equivocally. It needs the robust flow of the love of God in full flood to drown its efforts. It is the work of the devil to pretend that those lurking fears of the future are live and real. It is the work of Jesus, through the Holy Spirit, to remind us that they have been overcome. If, ultimately, the fear of death is taken from us, what fear can hold us in thrall? Grasping this truth is the object of our lives as Christians: Death has lost its sting. Fear has lost its supports. It has to crumble at the end when Christ is vindicated. But, oh, the damage it wreaks until then!

If we want to live fearlessly, our aims are to appropriate the depths of Jesus' love for us into our inner beings by the power of his Spirit. We need to be proactive. We have to throw all that we have into this struggle. We have to "set [our faces] like flint" (Isaiah 50:7), knowing in every fiber of our beings that we have the victory over fear and need to act accordingly every day.

At the height of the financial crisis in 2008–2009, I had to remind myself repeatedly of the need to fight fear, especially when it threatened to bring such colossal damage to the world. I was asked to speak to a group of business executives on how to respond to the frightening financial tsunami we were facing. I came back to Hebrews 12 and asked the question, "What is the bedrock of life?" The answer is that we stand on a solid rock "that cannot be shaken" (v. 28), which is Christ himself.

It was this knowledge—that there could never be a shaking so severe as to dislodge the life that Christ wanted to have in and through me—that sustained me day in and day out as the crashing markets threatened the whole world. This was one strand of my defense. I also consciously increased my times of prayer, even if I didn't know exactly how to pray.

Not Sink or Swim but Saved

My favorite painting, which hangs outside my study, is by a wonderful artist and friend, Roger Wagner. It shows Peter getting out of the storm-battered boat with one hand still tentatively holding on to the side. He hears the call of Jesus to come to him. With his other hand he reaches out to Jesus, as a child holding to the side of a swimming pool might reach out to her mother who is just out of reach.

I have often puzzled over this painting. Like so many of the stories in the Bible, the economy of the expression leaves questions unanswered. Peter, along with the other disciples in the boat, was terrified by the storm and by the appearance of Jesus. They thought Jesus was a ghost (Matthew 14:26). Of all the questions Peter could have asked of Jesus, why on earth did he say, "Lord, if it's you . . . tell me to come to you on the water" (v. 28)?

Surely it would have been simpler to ask Jesus to come closer and show himself to the disciples. Or, more sensibly still, to ask Jesus to calm the wind and the buffeting waves. What could be the benefit of Peter walking out to Jesus on the water?

It seems to me that Peter wanted proof of Jesus' presence, which would be validated through him; Peter wanted to be a part of the miracle.

But there is another possible explanation: Peter wanted to be where Jesus was. And it is Jesus' habit never to turn down anyone who wants to come to him, wherever he is and whatever the circumstances. So Jesus called, "Come" (v. 29), and Peter responded to what he believed was the voice of Jesus commanding him. He stood on the word of Jesus. He had to take a risk. The act of faith was not, as my picture depicts, Peter getting out of the boat but Peter responding to the voice of Jesus without guarantees.

At this point, he held on to the word. I suspect he could not see Jesus in the crashing waves and sea spray. All he had was what he thought was Jesus' voice calling him over. Then the waves overwhelmed him, as adversity can overwhelm us.

We are not guaranteed that our steps of faith will succeed. If faith were knowledge, it would not be faith, and there would be no need to trust. Trust is the way Jesus tests our relationship with him. And though Peter's trust diminished, he cried out, "Lord, save me!" And in response, Jesus reached out his hand and caught him.

Without Jesus, failure is a sink-or-swim situation. With Jesus, it's not sink or swim—it's *saved*. His hand reached out to Peter to save him. This is the huge comfort we have when we are facing the failure of a dream. Even if we embarked on the action, believing it was in response to Jesus' word, he doesn't leave us to sink under our failure, but to survive with his favor. This can only be understood as pure grace: actions taken in faith, even if they fail, will not cause his love for us to falter. Peter failed to do what he wanted to do. True. But Jesus prevailed in what he wanted to achieve: to show his grace whatever the circumstances might be.

Will you keep walking toward Jesus in the moments of life when you cannot see the way ahead? All of us face fear, failure, and disappointment in the course of our lives. You might be in the middle of an almighty failure right now, and you might feel as if you have burned all your bridges. But there is one bridge that will never burn: Jesus' grace saves again and again.

In 1854, Elisha Otis stood on a platform that had hoisted him above the New York crowd milling around him. He then instructed an axman to cut the rope that had hoisted him to that height. The crowd held their breath. To their astonishment he did not fall from his lofty position to the ground. Instead the platform dropped only a few feet. The new braking system he was demonstrating for his new safety lift locked into position and held the platform without the security of the rope. For the first time people were given the confidence to use what the Americans call an elevator.[7]

The rest is history. Otis elevators are now operating in most of the tallest buildings in the world. The equivalent of the entire population of the planet is moved up and down in buildings throughout the world every seventy-two hours. And we now have the possibility of an elevator one kilometer high as the result of technology developed from that first risk taken by Otis. But Otis himself did not think it was a risk. He knew he would be held safely by his automatic braking system. But the people around the prototype elevator gasped.

So it is with the Christian life. Yes, we take risks. Yes, we know that the rope needs to be cut. And yes, we may fall, sometimes quite spectacularly. But above all our failures and our falls is a God who is above and beyond all things. God, in Christ, has overcome all things. And he is here to catch us. He is the automatic braking system that can always be relied upon.

Jesus will not let us drop to the ground when we act in faith. We may stumble and fall, but we will not be lost or broken. As Psalm 37 puts it,

> The steps of a man are established by the LORD,
>> when he delights in his way;
> though he fall, he shall not be cast headlong,
>> for the LORD upholds his hand. (vv. 23–24 ESV)

That knowledge is the single most important determinant of my Christian life. I can never grasp its fullness. Many times—just as when I use an elevator—I presume that when I step out in faith there will be someone whose hand will reach out, as it did for Peter on the water, and catch my fall. And though I might sometimes fall further and harder than I hoped, God has never let me down.

What a God! By him I am loved, known, and called. Fear cannot break that bond. What a calling to follow him!

—— SEVEN ——

CALLED TO FOCUS

JESUS HAD A CALLING SPECIFICALLY FOR HIS DISCIPLES. HE gave them very precise, almost labored instructions on their missionary objectives: "Go nowhere among the Gentiles and do not go into any town of the Samaritans; but go rather to the lost sheep of the house of Israel" (Matthew 10:5–6 AMP).

I have puzzled over this teaching for many years. It seems strange that Jesus told the disciples *not* to spread the gospel among the Gentiles. Were they less important?

I have come to understand that this is a key teaching with regards to following the call of Jesus in our lives, and for one powerful reason: it deals with the restrictions on our callings. Jesus used the one word we hate more than most: *no*. But we will never mature in our callings until we have learned to say it ourselves.

Telling the disciples not to go to the Gentiles or Samaritans was not for racially prejudiced reasons. Jesus wanted to be sure that the disciples would not be distracted from their task, which was to minister specifically to the "lost sheep of the house of Israel." He then reinforced this singular objective by insisting that they not take any extras: "no bag for the journey or extra shirt or sandals or a staff" (v. 10 NIV). He set clear objectives and removed the clutter that could distract. Priorities are key to calling.

Clutter is a big issue in modern living, and as Christians, we need to deal with it regularly. There is just too much *stuff*. There's always stuff on our smartphones, stuff in our inboxes, stuff clogging up our attics, our lives. "Simplify your life, and your calling will be clearer," a wise friend once said to me.

I am a terrible packer. I have a "what if" bag about which my family teases me mercilessly. It almost always leads to excess baggage charges. It has every imaginable extra that might be required for the journey. I do not travel lightly—sometimes a pair of skiing gloves makes its way on safari in Africa! I had a conversation with the adventurer Bear Grylls about packing before he climbed Everest. Bear's simple comment was that, if you are climbing Everest, you don't need unnecessary clutter and weight. You need to stay focused. You have to declutter.

So what about us? Like the disciples, we don't need unnecessary clutter. And typically for us, clutter equals distractions. There are many times when we have to say no, however hard it is, if we are to avoid diluting God's call. As *The Message* translation puts it: "All I want is for you to be able to develop a way of life in which you can spend plenty of time together with the Master without a lot of distractions" (1 Corinthians 7:35).

DRIVEN TO DISTRACTION

We can be distracted so easily in this technologically driven, hyper-connected, always-on society. Jesus' teaching ensures that we fulfill our callings and are not tempted to devise other, often more interesting tasks. It's worth going through a few of the biggest distractions.

1. DISTRACTED BY MISSION CREEP

Jesus had a specific call on the disciples' lives, as he does on ours, and he wants to guard against our dissipating this call. Often logic would dictate other courses of action: "Why not go to the Gentile cities on a mission? Don't they need Jesus?" But logic can be wrong: mission creep is a danger to most callings and Christian ministries.

There is always a temptation to widen our objectives through ill-discipline, a failure to focus, or a reluctance to prioritize. I have seen many people waste their callings by adding to them. But there is an imperative "Do not go!" in Jesus' instructions.

We are often tempted to try to do more than we are called to do. Whenever I question such additions, people tend to reply that there is "great need" to create some additional activity. And there usually is, just as there was a need for the Gentiles to hear the gospel. But their time had not yet come. And the need is not the call. There are many needs in the world today. We cannot satisfy all of them. God knows our needs and those of the world. He also knows the right timing for our actions.

Some distractions are legitimate—but only if they are part of the overall calling. Jesus was apparently distracted from his objective in the story of Jairus's daughter found in Mark's gospel. While Jesus was on his way to Jairus's house to heal the man's daughter, a woman who had been bleeding for twelve years sought out Jesus and touched his cloak, believing that she would be healed (Mark 5:21–32). It was legitimate to stop and deal with her request, as healing was part of his primary purpose and his specific calling. It appeared to those around him as a distraction. But to Jesus it was determinative of his mission.

There are times, however, when we are drawn away from a clear purpose only to slip into a side stream. This stream may be a good cause and flow to fruitful outcomes, but it is not where we should be. There are few diversions so potent as the worthwhile side stream. It seems legitimate and appears to bear fruit, so we are likely to diverge. Often this occurs with highly motivated people, or businesses that are successful, or growing churches. New ventures and opportunities with seeming legitimacy divert them from the main stream. The side stream might be refreshing, but it is not the river.

I think of the catastrophe that hit LEGO when it decided to move away from its basic business of giving young children the opportunity to use their hands and minds to make interesting constructions. The key desire of the original owner was that LEGOs would be an educational, time-consuming, and engaging activity for children. It was just too easy for the new management to decide to add video games, clothing, and theme parks to the suite of toys. The diversification seemed like a good idea, but it was a huge distraction.

Video games in particular are more entertainment than education and require instant responses. The key objective of enabling a child to take time to do something was lost. In the end, the company practically collapsed. They then redesigned their product offering and went back to their original bricks. What appeared a legitimate distraction almost destroyed the destiny of a company.[1]

2. Distracted by distraction

Of course, it's not just mission creep that can distract us. T. S. Eliot wrote the words "distracted from distraction by distraction,"[2] which captures something of the spirit of our age. While every age has its measure of distractions (and T. S. Eliot was clearly concerned with those of his), the potential for distraction seems to have exploded in our times beyond anything that could previously have been imagined.

Distraction is everywhere, and more worryingly, there is an increased desire for continuous distraction from real life. It is as if our attention spans have shortened and it is becoming harder and harder for us to focus on one thing for any length of time. But focus matters. And it is hard to fulfill our callings without it.

Stimulus addiction is the great addiction of our age. The pressing need to have constant digital stimuli—whether to text, tweet, check Facebook, post photos on Instagram, send e-mails, surf the Internet, Skype, Periscope, or watch television—is apparently uncontrollable and insatiable. And now all of these can be done on the go wherever we are from one handheld device.

The precise claim of a distraction is that it requires very little concentration. That is why Twitter, Snapchat, and Instagram can be such a diversion. We can absentmindedly scroll away to see what snappy thought grabs our attention. We linger for a moment and then speed on. Twitter is a wonderful tool, but its use needs to be guarded. Even good things can become curses through over-indulgence. The world is no longer at our feet; it is terrifyingly and dizzyingly at our fingertips.

How strange that we now talk about TV, Twitter, and the like as digital "feeds." Are they feeding us as human beings? Are they nourishing and strengthening our humanity? Recent studies have shown that Internet addiction may produce just as much plaque on the brain as do alcohol, marijuana, and cocaine addictions.[3] Digital distraction, if untamed, can make us numb to God.

3. DISTRACTED BY THE NEED FOR INSTANT GRATIFICATION

Driving through London, I notice the enormous billboards at big junctions promising that if we commit to a particular broadband package, we will have supersonically quick Internet connections. We are persuaded into a deal because of its speed—as if speed equals efficiency. Have we made speed an idol? The level of irritation we feel when, for some reason, our laptops do not open a new Internet page at lightning speed is an indication of how far we have mutated in the last decade or so. It's almost as if Wi-Fi capacity is a God-given right, and it is deeply irritating if service providers don't deliver at the breakneck, mind-blowing speed to which we have become accustomed.

Snatching food, information, and images at such speed is not conducive to hearing God. The pace of our age is often out of sync with the rhythms of God's timing. If we succumb too much to the pace surrounding us, we will miss his subtle signs.

At times God does deliver quickly, but it is far more likely that he will take time, longing to develop a relationship of trust with us by interacting in real time. God is not a search engine. His replies tend not to be instantaneous. It is easy to expect God to identify our destinies fast—and then to get on and fulfill them just as quickly. We want immediate answers and instant gratification. But sometimes slower answers, a longer wait, a deeper wrestle, and further reflection bring more nourishing outcomes and are closer to the heart of God for whom continuing relationships matter more than anything else.

If we're hungry, it's easy to shove a ready meal in the microwave, press six minutes, and be done. Maybe occasional slow cooking would remind us of the rhythms of life not lived in the fast lane.

Likewise, it can be tempting to fall prey to short-termism, particularly where money is concerned. If we "live now, pay later"—perhaps by incurring unwieldy debt—there will, of course, come a time when we have to pay. Our generation is one that says, "Why trade enjoyment today for what may not be around tomorrow?" And so we become distracted by the immediate at the expense of the long term. This attitude has a colossal consequence in the level of debt that society is incurring under the erroneous assumption that it doesn't need to be paid back yet. The problem is that anxiety over money distracts us from our callings. Money always holds that danger as we balance a pragmatic and wise approach with the peril of being seduced by the right salary for the wrong job.

4. DISTRACTED BY OUR OWN BAD CHOICES

"But your iniquities have separated you from your God; your sins have hidden his face from you, so that he will not hear" (Isaiah 59:2).

I was speaking to a young skiing instructor named Anton, who was searching for meaning in his life and unsure of where the future lay for him. At one point in our conversation we somehow got on the subject of sin. He looked blankly at me. No, he said, he didn't think he had any sins and was not really ashamed of anything. Although, he admitted, he had made many mistakes. But then, don't we all? I realized in that conversation that the concept of sin—acts that cut us off from God—has been airbrushed from the consciences of a generation.

But our sins, our bad habits, our wrong choices—whatever you want to call them—are so often our main distractions, and we must face them to be set free from their shackles.

Carl Jung, one of the fathers of psychoanalysis, was once asked to comment on the people who came to see him for help. He said that the majority were not suffering from mental illness but were "stuck." They had become trapped in patterns of behavior from which they could not escape or in a groove of anxiety.[4]

Christians can be like that. We get trapped in cycles and patterns of sin that drag us down and rob us of the Spirit's movement in our lives. But the Spirit changes us. He makes all things new and gives us just the right push to keep us going. Jesus wants to give us life in all its fullness (John 10:10). He does not plan for us to be stuck in a behavioral rut from which there is no obvious escape.

But when we sin, we are cut off from God and his face is hidden from us. Sin is the real reason we get stuck. Sin is not simply a mistake, as my friend Anton was inclined to think. It is not something that affects only him.

Some say that the prayer God answers the quickest is, "Lord, show me what I have done wrong." Normally a plethora of wrong choices come to mind, and we recognize where we have gone astray.

We need to lay off doing that which we know to be wrong. It's not an easy process, and there is no shortcut. It requires an act of the will. If I have been turning in false expense forms to my employer, all I have to do is stop. If I am lying about the progress of the report that is expected of me, I need to stop and dare to live a life of honesty. God sees what you are doing, even if your boss does not. And God will honor you for the honest choices you make. There is no equivocation about it—if it is wrong, stop it. That's it. Courageous integrity is what we are all called to.

Sometimes, however strong our willpower, we won't get off the starting block without help. That is when the Holy Spirit provides the power to get us going again. But we must turn to him for help.

A DESTINY DESTROYED BY DISTRACTION

Samson had one great God-given task, a clear calling. The prophecy had been given to his parents before he was even born: Samson would take the lead in delivering Israel from the oppression of the Philistines (Judges 13:5).

There it was: his destiny laid out for him. And to fulfill this calling, God equipped him with extraordinary strength to do awesome feats, just as he equips all of us to fulfill our callings and destinies.

But Samson had great weaknesses—girls, gambling, grumbling, and goading being some of them. His self-serving attraction to women was his downfall time after time, until it killed him.

One day he fell in love with a beautiful woman named Delilah. Unbeknown to Samson, however, Delilah had been bribed by Samson's enemies, the Philistines, who sought to destroy him and the Israelites. Three times she pressed him for the key to his strength, and three times he resisted her. The fourth time, when she questioned his love for her, Samson let his guard down and told her the reason for his strength: "If my head were shaved, my strength would leave me, and I would become as weak as any other man" (Judges 16:17). And thus, "after putting him to sleep on her lap, she called for someone to shave off the seven braids of his hair. . . . And his strength left him" (v. 19).

It was the persistence of the enemy that really did Samson in. He resisted telling Delilah the truth time and again, but eventually he was worn down. His lust for the wrong women was the weakness that gave Satan a foothold from which he could launch repeated attacks. Even the strongest callings can be whittled away by distractions if we allow them to go unchecked.

Samson let his guard down twice—first, in telling Delilah his secret, and second, in allowing himself to be "put to sleep" (lulled by sexual intimacy). But this is the warning: we must beware of being asleep when we should be alert to temptation. Beware of being lulled and led astray "on the lap" of something that gives temporary comfort or recreational satisfaction. Flirtation, flattery, compulsion, whim—we all know the slippery feel of these things. Beware, because this is a downward slope, and Samson slipped. Delilah coaxed Samson to sleep, knowing that she could take full advantage of him when he was vulnerable. And we, too, can slip easily.

Sure enough, Samson's hair was cut and God's strength left him. And as if that was not cruel enough, the Philistines gouged out his eyes and imprisoned him.

In *Samson Agonistes*, the great commentary on the life of Samson by John Milton, we see the agony of a man who undid himself through the dangerous distractions that seduced him, missing out on his divine calling:

> Promise was that I
> Should Israel from Philistian yoke deliver!
> Ask for this great Deliverer now, and find him
> Eyeless in Gaza, at the mill with slaves,
> Himself in bonds under Philistian yoke.
> Yet stay; let me not rashly call in doubt
> Divine prediction. What if all foretold
> Had been fulfilled but through mine own default?
> Whom have I to complain of but myself?[5]

And yet—with our God there is always an "and yet"—this incredible thing happened: his hair grew back again (Judges 16:22). As his hair started to grow and his strength started to return, so did all the promises of the call on his life.

However distracted we may have become, whether through

default or our own fault, the supreme, redeeming grace of God is given to us. With God there is never a lost-and-gone-forever condition. His grace allows us to recover even from the worst lapses. He never abandons us because of our failings but constantly holds out the offer of restoring the source of our strength—however badly we might have messed up.

Samson called out to God, "O Lord God, please remember me and please strengthen me only this once, O God" (v. 28 ESV). The monumental destruction of the temple happened, and the monumental distractions of his life ended. As the building collapsed and killed three thousand Philistines, he was killed as well—*but the people of God survived.* God's ultimate purposes were fulfilled.

Like Samson's, our callings are not only personal. All of our paths work together to demonstrate God's goodness on earth. If our callings come from God, then they do not die with us. Legacy begins not when we die but now, as we fulfill our callings, linking with the other members of our communities or churches. Just as our callings build upon the ways in which previous generations have responded to God, so do we lay the foundation for the future work of others. In the words of Sir Isaac Newton, "If I have seen further, it is by standing on the shoulders of Giants."[6]

STEPS TO DEAL WITH DISTRACTION

At the eleventh hour, Samson reconnected with God. Let us now look at some practical steps we can take to reconnect with God, even as our lives seem to be crumbling around us.

1. METANOIA: TURNING AROUND

Every decision to start afresh begins with one word, *metanoia*, which is the Greek word for repentance. It means "to turn around and face in the opposite direction." We cannot unstick ourselves. The first step to leading a great life of purpose is to say sorry and to do something about it—that is, to try not to get stuck again. *Metanoia* is a huge word, and it is the source of a guilt-free life. This word summarizes our response to Jesus' death and is the core of a fulfilled life. It recognizes that Christ died not only to bring forgiveness of our sins, but to do something even more amazing and positive: to reckon us as righteous in the eyes of God.

Regret is a negative and emotional reaction to personal past acts and behavior. During a meeting in which we had tense discussions on the nature of a particular contract, the lawyer lost his temper. His behavior was understandable, as it was the middle of the night. He told me that he regretted his overreaction, but he had no sense that he needed to put anything right. He was simply expressing his feeling, and he quite possibly felt better for getting it off his chest.

Remorse is a deeper regret, which tends to include shame. A coworker once told me that she was filled with remorse for having behaved badly toward a colleague. The feelings were deep and authentic—but I don't know if she ever acted on them.

Repentance is more than regret and remorse. It requires action: we turn around. Repentance is much richer in content and more powerful to liberate us. It is not a psychological process meant to relieve our actions. In Romans 2:4, we read that "God's kindness is meant to lead you to repentance" (ESV). Repentance prompts us to apologize—both to the people we have wronged (if this is possible) and crucially to God. It is against God, in all cases of wrongdoing, that we have sinned. God alone is able to forgive, and when he hears the word *sorry*, he rushes to reinstate the person seeking forgiveness. This is his crowning work on the cross. Even in the midst of his crucifixion, Christ spoke words of forgiveness and grace over his executioners: "Father, forgive them, for they do know not what they are doing" (Luke 23:34). Forgiveness is there, just waiting for us to accept it.

Every year, my church hosts a leadership conference in the Royal Albert Hall. In 2015, one of the speakers was the preacher to the papal household, Father Raniero Cantalamessa. In an authoritative message Father Raniero explained how a misunderstanding of *metanoia* led to an overemphasis on guilt and a failure to see the majestic, positive value of turning in a new direction. Dwelling on the sins of the past has contributed to pessimism about the faith rather than a liberating realization of the salvation in Christ. It is this salvation that lies at the heart of the good news—that a genuinely repentant person can leave the past behind and move with renewed confidence and joy into a future free from guilt. No calling is complete without a true understanding of *metanoia*.

Repentance, then, gives us freedom to fulfill our callings without the burden of the past destroying the open spaces of life to which the Spirit calls us. To repent and say sorry is a transformative act of redemption that centers our lives on God.

Given the enormous redemptive potential of the simple but compelling word *sorry*, I'm always struck by how difficult it is to say. The principal reason is that we have no way in the work environment to deal with repentance. Every mistake is seemingly fatal. If the CEO makes a mistake and the company performs badly, the CEO is fired. But Jesus is not an unforgiving shareholder. He knows that we will make mistakes. He knows that we will do wrong. And with this knowledge, he provides a way for us to be restored if only we confess our wrong choices, apologize, and resolve to start afresh. The blood of Jesus is the mode of our forgiveness and is always effective. We contribute nothing to this gracious intervention. Without recognition of our need for open and honest channels of communication with God, we are unable to hear his voice as he confirms each step in our callings.

I was recently on an airplane between business meetings, jet lagged and stressed out by work, listening to Hillsong United's song "Beautiful Exchange."[7] One verse in particular stood out to me, as it spoke of Jesus "trading" his life for my offenses. He took my blame and the curse of death that came with it and traded it for his perfection.

Trading is what we do in business, swapping a product for money.

But we trade in equal values. We sell a product for the amount we believe it to be worth. And yet *this* trade, in which Jesus willingly exchanged his own exalted life for my dirt and sin and muck, is not a trade that any financier I know of would ever make. Yet this is what the song appropriately called a "beautiful exchange."

The effect on me was overwhelming. There is real power in understanding the idea of the great exchange that Jesus secured on the cross. It is beautiful beyond description. He took my messed-up life and exchanged it for a life mended by grace. He will do the same for you—and for anyone who asks. He takes the worthlessness of our lives and makes them worthwhile.

2. MODE CHANGE

So much of our time is spent in output: texting, tweeting, uploading our latest news. It is therefore so easy to slip into this way of communicating with God. We need to set aside time for input. A simple way is to say to yourself, "Switch now." This could be your code, as it is for me, that it is time to slow down, switch out of transmit mode and into receive mode, and begin to listen to God.

Jesus himself withdrew to silent places to be alone and recharge his spiritual batteries by spending time in the presence of his Father (Matthew 14:23). These are the words he speaks to us, not just two thousand years ago, but now, today: "Come to me. Get away with me and you'll recover your life. I'll show you how to take a real rest. Walk with me and work with me—watch how I do it. Learn the unforced rhythms of grace. I won't lay anything heavy or ill-fitting on you. Keep company with me and you'll learn to live freely and lightly" (Matthew 11:28–30 THE MESSAGE). In a world weighed down by busyness and noise, we need to recover the ability to recognize the rhythms of life.

We cannot hope to find, and then fulfill, our callings if we do not consciously receive God's message. Following a calling is a partnership with God—which means we need to take the time to listen.

One of the first spiritual disciplines I learned when my faith came alive was to have a time of prayer each day. I have tried to do this most mornings for the last forty years. This special time is made up of the following:

+ **READING THE SCRIPTURES.** I cannot recommend more highly *The Bible in One Year* commentary by Nicky and Pippa Gumbel.[8] It's brilliant in its insights and a great help in starting the day. It's also an invaluable way to get to know the Word of God. Every day it encourages the reader to look at a passage in depth and to take the time to hear what God might be saying through it. In withdrawing from the problems of the day and committing time to the Scriptures, I find a new perspective that—while coming from something apparently unrelated—gives me insight into the issues that I face.

+ **PRAYER.** This is a time of worship and request in which we lay before him those issues on our hearts. "Do not be anxious about anything, but in every situation, by prayer and petition, with thanksgiving, present your requests to God" (Philippians 4:6). Thanksgiving and requests are conjoined twins. It is for this reason that I now keep a prayer journal. I try to write in it each day both my many thanksgivings and my specific prayers. I have found excitement in going over the previous months and ticking the number of prayers answered. Of course, sometimes prayers don't get answered—or maybe they are answered with a no—which can be hard. But going through the process of writing them down has helped me learn how to embrace even these negative answers. Whether God's answer is yes, no, or not yet, all things work together for the good for those who love the Lord and are called to his purpose (Romans 8:28).

+ **SILENCE.** This is key to being in receive mode, and it is often the most difficult part! Silence means just waiting on God.

It is the time when I try as best I can to stop my praying and supplication and allow God to be who he is. A wise pastor once told me that when deciding whom to marry, the greatest test was to find someone with whom you could share silences. At the time, I received the advice with amused indifference, but after many years of marriage I now know this to be true of all relationships. There is something about silence that is more intimate than any words.

3. MEDITATE

Silence is not just for our quiet times, however. Allowing ourselves to get away from all distractions at regular intervals is vital for healthy spirituality. But silence can also be quite scary. Sam Wells, the leader of St Martin-in-the-Fields Church in Trafalgar Square, talks of the "terrifying intimacy" that comes from daring ourselves to sit in silence with God.[9] Are we afraid of what we might hear?

In July 2014, the results of a fascinating experiment were published in the United States. Hundreds of volunteers had been placed in sparsely furnished rooms with their belongings (including phones and pens) put away, and they had fifteen minutes in which to be alone, silent, with their own thoughts and nothing to distract them. To take the experiment to a new level, they were given the option to self-administer an electric shock if they found the silence and stillness too difficult. The results were astonishing.

"What is striking is that simply being alone with their thoughts was apparently so aversive that it drove many participants to self-administer an electric shock that they had earlier said they would pay to avoid," said the investigators at the University of Virginia.[10] This is a sobering discovery.

Are we really so afraid that if we sit still we will go to pieces?

Nothing will transform your life as much as hearing and heeding God's whispering voice. It was the still small voice of God that turned Elijah's heart in the midst of his despair (1 Kings 19:12–13).

It is the greatest blessing of every Christian to have the opportunity to listen for and to obey the whispers of God. But unless we dare to be still and quiet and unplugged, we will not be able to hear him. Confirmation of our callings requires daily nurturing. It's not a one-off agreement between us and God; it's nuanced and relational. We need to keep hearing from God on a regular basis throughout our Christian journeys.

Though the devil shouts quite a bit, God rarely does. He nudges us, impresses us when he wants to say something. In order to hear a whisper, it is necessary to lean in, to draw like two lovers on a park bench. When we whisper, we strain for understanding and hang on to every word. And that is what God so desperately wants to do with us. Without space and silence, away from distractions, we will not absorb and appropriate the person of Christ into our lives. Growing in kindness, humility, and grace and learning to look out for others are things that seldom happen overnight; we grow over time with practice and reflection.

During a time of worship in church I sensed God speaking to me about the need to make a decision at work that would require courage I didn't think I had. I heard him say the name *Caleb*. As we discussed in chapter 2, Caleb had gone into Canaan when the Israelites were looking to settle in the promised land, and he had reported back, "I know there are giants out there, but surely we can do this" (Numbers 13:30, author's paraphrase). Caleb was a can-do person, and this was just the word I needed to face some major changes.

As soon as the worship ended, someone whom I had never met before came up to me and offered to pray for me. Of course, I agreed. He offered an affirming prayer that spoke to my heart. Then I asked him his name.

"Caleb," he replied.

What an encouragement!

The Spirit of God whispers to us while the devil wails and screams, trying to distract us. Whom are we going to listen to? Let us listen to the Word of God; he may nudge us to forgive a colleague at work or be kind to someone who needs assurance. God whispers as we walk through life, so we need to be open, willing, obedient, and connected in order to hear him. Let's not miss out on his words of life that so sustain and embolden us for the purposes he has given us.

In his intriguing book *Silence—A Christian History*, Diarmaid MacCulloch described how the church has negotiated noise and silence, from the early boisterous enthusiasm of Israel to the monastic renewal of silence in worship.[11] He pointed to the effectiveness of the silent witness of Christ on the cross and the quiet prayers of Jesus in secluded places. There is, of course, a time to be voluble and a time to say nothing. We know how to do the former well; it would be good to master the latter. We all need to learn a new way of listening rather than speaking in our polyphonic digital world.

4. LISTEN WITH YOUR EYES

I remember a moment when my wife was trying to talk to me while I was on my iPhone. She asked whether I was listening, to which I replied, "Yes," and to prove it I repeated the last phrase she had said. But that was not the point.

"Echolalia!" she replied.

I had not heard the word before, but I later discovered that it referred to the repeating back of what someone had just said. I was echoing back to her what I had heard without any real human involvement. Then she gave me a shake and said, "Will you listen with your eyes?"

She was quite right. Listening involves the whole body; it can't be outsourced to the ears only. The whole person is involved in communicating, hence the call to listen with my eyes, register contact, show engagement, and avoid distraction.

Zacchaeus is a good example of someone who concentrated on Jesus with his whole person. He wanted to see who Jesus was, so he climbed up a tree to get a good view. And because he was so attentive, he heard Jesus' call to him. Interestingly, upon seeing Jesus and hearing him speak, Zacchaeus was immediately convicted of his past sins and determined to change his future into a better one (Luke 19:8). Isn't this so often the case with us too? It is only when we dare to be still and listen to God that our sins become apparent. We are then able to repent and start in a new direction. First we must learn to listen properly, and then we can act. Listening and acting result from living in connection with God.

When torrential rainfall hit the United Kingdom a few years ago, the swollen rivers should have had clear runs to the sea to prevent flooding. But the rivers had silted up and had not been dredged. When the rains came, the river channels could not contain the water. So, too, with us: if we want to hear clearly, we have to take steps to dredge the junk and distractions out of our lives—the sins that pile up and silt up—in order for the Spirit to flow freely.

5. SET BOUNDARIES

I am totally wired to this digital age, and I love it, yet I need to recognize where technology has an unhealthy hold on my life. We should consider applying Jesus' views on fasting to our gadgets, perhaps by taking time out—for example on a Sunday or for an hour or two each day—from responding in any way. The difficulty of doing so, if you are a habitual user, tells its own story. Who holds whom becomes clear. A break from television, texting, e-mails, and the Internet for a fixed period is a way to break a habit and recover control of your life.

Jesus asks us to fast to help change our appetites. He needs to change our desires and attachments and reveal what it is that distracts us from his presence. So we stop allowing Facebook and Twitter to force-feed us and invite the Word of God to nourish us. Of course, I am not saying that we can do without these essentials of modern living (if for no other reason than many of us have our

Bibles and notebooks on our smartphones!), but when we are distracted, we need the perspective brought by fasting.

When I left the bank where I was chairman and started a new project on my own, the greatest stress was that the telephone did not ring. I felt lost, watching it every few seconds and leaping to answer every call. I was also mortified if my friends did not respond immediately to my texts and calls. I then started switching the phone off for increasingly long periods to help break the dependence pattern. I had some success—not a lot—but my intentions were good!

A few years ago, I attended a lunch in the City where the speaker was Arianna Huffington. She explained her attempts to prevent burnout at the *Huffington Post*, which she part owns. She has insisted that all work e-mails are switched off when the person leaves work and should not be switched on until the next time they are on duty. In this way she reminds employees to have lives outside of work.

I try not to take my smartphone to bed with me. Somehow not having the device with me at the end of the day is a salutary cut-off point. But most important, it preserves the time with my wife. Mind you, I have failed to extend this seeming virtue to watching television in bed!

6. RESIST TEMPTATION

Having turned around in repentance, switched from transmit to receive, and listened for a word from God, we combat distraction by actively resisting temptation. Samson failed to do so, and he was drawn away from his calling. We, too, can be drawn toward fantasies and delusions; temptations are common, though not all lead to sin. But we need to regularly practice resisting through the power of the Spirit to ensure that temptation doesn't dictate our lives.

Three distractions in particular may try to derail your calling: gold (lusting after money), girls/guys (lusting after sex), and glory (lusting after power). These temptations should be dealt with by fight and flight. Meditating on Jesus Christ and his crucifixion is helpful when we desire power at the expense of God's own glory. The athlete who enjoys the glory of a great win is right to enjoy it, provided he realizes that what he has, he received from God. But when we fall into the trap of drawing power to ourselves and enjoying vainglorious reflections, then it's time to confess and to start on a new path.

7. STAY CONNECTED

I remember the exact moment I realized the importance of staying connected in my relationship with Jesus if I was not to lose sight of his calling. I was sitting near the front in the O_2 Arena in London listening to T. D. Jakes, one of the most skillful preachers of our time. He was telling the story of Abraham in a resonant, pounding voice, while mopping his brow with a large hanky. Simply put, he pointed out that if Abraham had been obedient to the voice of God to take Isaac to Mount Moriah and sacrifice him there, but *had failed to listen to God's continued voice*, then Isaac would have been killed as God had originally asked. Quite an arresting thought when one considers the consequences of that act: no people of Israel, no Christian church.

But Abraham stayed connected and heard the Lord speak again, with instructions to untie Isaac. And then, in what appears to be a literal distraction, Abraham saw a ram caught in a bush. It was the perfect substitute for the sacrifice, and it appeared at exactly the right time. The ram would have wandered up the hill and become tangled in the thicket precisely when Abraham needed to know that God had not only spoken but provided an alternative. His son would not be sacrificed.

God doesn't always give his instructions in full at the outset; if he did, we would be clamoring for the blueprint. Trying to live on yesterday's manna can lead to scary consequences. The nature of God's great provision to the people of Israel in the desert was that there was enough food for only one day—they had to trust that God would provide tomorrow's manna when it was needed. God calls us to walk by faith, to wait for his voice, and not to be distracted. We cannot afford to lose connectivity.

Our relationship with Jesus is a dynamic one. He speaks often, revealing only in part, testing our obedience, and then disclosing his intentions step by step. We need to keep ourselves free from distraction, in a position to hear him, ready at all times to obey.

EIGHT

CALLED TO PERSEVERE

ON JANUARY 14, 2015, AFTER NEARLY THREE WEEKS OF exhausting and relentless climbing, Kevin Jorgeson and Tommy Caldwell reached the top of the El Capitan rock formation in Yosemite National Park. They made history as the first people to free climb the sheer Dawn Wall—climbing without aids, using ropes only to secure themselves when they inevitably and repeatedly fell. At three thousand feet high and composed of thirty-two sections—some of which are among the hardest climbs in the world all by themselves—the Dawn Wall had long been considered an impossible endeavor among the mountaineering community.

For nineteen days Jorgeson and Caldwell slept between climbing sessions in tents suspended hundreds of feet into the air. They repeated the same moves over and over as they tried to conquer the Dawn Wall's different sections. Again and again they sliced their hands and fingers open on the razor-sharp rock, making advances of only a few inches. Scaling the imposing Dawn Wall had been Caldwell and Jorgeson's goal for a long time, and they had spent eight years preparing for it.

Using social media to communicate, they continually updated their progress. The world watched and waited with bated breath as they conquered this colossal rock face.[1]

Part of the reason the story got so much attention, Jorgeson guessed, is that people can relate to elements of the journey. "It's a big dream, it requires teamwork and determination and commitment," said Jorgeson. "And those aren't climbing-specific attributes. Those are common to everybody, whether you're trying to write a book or climb a rock."[2]

At one point, when he was suffering, Caldwell sent out a message saying: "Razor sharp holds ripped both the tape and the skin right off my fingers. As disappointing as this is, I'm learning new levels of patience, perseverance and desire. I'm not giving up. I will rest. I will try again. I will succeed."[3]

The specific objective is irrelevant, he said, but both climbers hope that their experience might inspire others to ask themselves: "What's my Dawn Wall?"[4]

FACING OUR MOUNTAINS

What is your Dawn Wall? Christians all seek the kingdom (Matthew 6:33)—and, as a result, we find ourselves on a journey of refinement. But within this macro-objective lie our own micro-objectives, given to us by God. We long to buy in to something larger than ourselves, a cause that transcends our own day-to-day endeavors and lifts up our eyes.

"Lead me to the rock that is higher than I." That is the prayer of David in Psalm 61:2. It's a prayer of longing for something more, something bigger than the introspective self.

What goal in your life is so important that it would inspire you to prepare for eight years? Do you have a passion to write a novel or set up your own business, or is it your goal to take on a sporting challenge or a fantastic expedition? What might God be calling you to that will take months, years, or even decades of perseverance to see come to fruition?

Each of us has a Dawn Wall. For some, it is an abiding passion from childhood that never leaves; for others, it develops as we grow or get to know ourselves better, and as God guides us. Some rock faces are more imposing than others, but all require, as Jorgeson said, "determination and commitment." Let us look at how we may face our Dawn Walls with courage, faith, and most of all, perseverance. Whereas Jorgeson and Caldwell relied on tiny, slippery footholds in the rock, we can rely on a God who makes our feet "like the feet of a deer" and "causes [us] to stand on the heights" (Psalm 18:33).

1. LIFT UP YOUR EYES

I am dispirited by a generation whose heads are bowed downward. Wherever we go, whether walking in the street or sitting in a restaurant, waiting in line or walking in the park, we are staring down at our smartphones. We spend our time disengaged from the abundant life that surrounds us. Of course, I understand the vital importance of these devices that have transformed our lives. But what I see is a picture of introspection and self-containment. It is as if all sources of wisdom and revelation, as well as knowledge and social interaction, come from handheld devices. When I see this, a cry forms within me. It is that of Psalm 24: "Lift up your heads, you gates; be lifted up, you ancient doors, that the King of glory may come in" (v. 7).

We need to look up. To rise higher. To aspire to the One who is above it all.

It is God who leads us upward, to that which is bigger and higher and beyond our own abilities. One of the great complaints of this age is that there is no real sense of a higher purpose—that we're just muddling through life, staring at our hands. But there are mountains to conquer and mountains to destroy, if only we would look. Mountains of corruption, poverty, and trafficking, as well as the mountains of greed and depression. Then there are the mountains of achievement and adventure—the challenges that we, both as individuals and as communities, are called to confront. We just have to lift our eyes up and away from ourselves.

While those two climbers were at the rock face, all they could see was the small area in front of their noses. But during the time of preparation and dreaming, Jorgeson and Caldwell would have spent days and weeks sitting at the bottom of the wall, staring up and taking in the spectacle. They would have held that image in their minds' eyes, even as they were confronted with the minutiae of tiny holds and fingers that had been sliced.

God called Zechariah to lead the people of Jerusalem to rebuild the temple, which lay in ruins. It was a call to get the people to look away from their own preoccupations and work together. The people were depressed and downcast; Zechariah was called to lift their hearts and show them God's vision.

Zechariah knew that in this great task of rebuilding the temple there was one unchallengeable fact: "'Not by might nor by power, but by my Spirit,' says the LORD Almighty" (Zechariah 4:6). He needed to encourage the people to look up and to see that what seemed impossible was indeed possible only with God.

2. LOOK TOGETHER

Very rarely will we be called to climb mountains alone. Often our endeavors will be collective, as we play small parts in big visions. Perhaps as a church we buy in to a goal that we work at together: an initiative to alleviate extreme poverty, eradicate human trafficking, build homes in developing countries, set up a school, or bring the good news of Jesus to the neighbors on our street. These objectives may well be outside our comfort zones. Alpha, pioneered by my friend Nicky Gumbel, has been one of the buy ins of my life. I chair the board, which keeps me close to the nitty-gritty, but the overall vision is so much bigger than anything I could achieve on my own.

When we buy in to something greater than ourselves, we discover that the Spirit accompanies us through the highs and lows on the journey and that others are on the same journey. We are not on our own. We share in the aspirations and achievements of those who are pulling in the same direction. Jorgeson and Caldwell climbed the Dawn Wall together, but they also had an enormous support crew who made the whole thing possible, making sure they had food and a secure bed each night. The same was true for those Zechariah organized to rebuild the temple. Each worked in his particular place at the wall, but all worked collectively, and they saw a common vision taking shape.

3. SEARCH FOR DIFFERENT ROUTES

A good friend was staying with us on vacation one year. During the week, he needed to go to another part of Switzerland to visit some friends. We showed him a map of the area and the route to take around Lake Geneva. He thought there was no reason to follow our instructions and instead decided to travel as the crow flies, which he assumed would be the shorter route. However, the road soon dead-ended in front of the mighty Alps. He could not cross them. He discovered, several thousand years after Hannibal, that these obstacles required a retreat. And so he returned to our chalet dispirited by these mountains that do not give way merely because we wish to cross them.

I was once asked to advise a major European airline client, which was facing great challenges, on the future of the airline industry. A new dynamic chief executive had taken over at the airline, and I asked him what was the most difficult management issue he faced. It was the mind-sets of his colleagues—they would focus on a mountain but could not see a path through it. He saw it as his task to show them a wider vista. In a memorable conversation, he went on to say, "I have to persuade my management team that what they *think* is an impenetrable brick wall is in fact a wall made of papier-mache. I have to teach them to break through and see that the 'brick wall' is actually no obstacle at all. If they manage that, there will be no restraint to their creativity."

Obstacles can inspire creativity. God has given us the imagination to think out of the box. I think of the friends of the paralyzed man in chapter 2 of Mark's gospel. They could have decided their Dawn Wall was too big: Jesus was surrounded by impenetrable crowds, their friend was far too heavy to carry, and even if they did manage to get through, Jesus might not heal him. There were lots of mountains to overcome and every good reason to give up on the whole idea. But they were persistent and innovative. They decided to cut a hole in the roof and lower their friend down (Mark 2:4). Those looking on would think they were mad! But they got what they wanted, and their friend was healed.

4. SPEAK TO THE MOUNTAINS

Living by the Spirit means nothing can stand in the way of the purposes of the Lord. As Zechariah said, "What are you, mighty mountain? Before Zerubbabel you will become level ground" (Zechariah 4:7).

All mountains have one thing in common: *they are big.* They loom large and cast dark shadows: illness, opposition, stress, disappointment, bereavement, persecution, fear of the unknown. Mountains can stop us in our tracks. They can force us to rethink and replan. Their size drives us to feel insignificant and hopeless. But we need to know that God is bigger than they are. We are supported by someone mightier than the mountains we face. *Our weaknesses are no obstacle to God's power.*

God is able to use the weakest person as long as he or she relies on his Spirit to perform at a higher level. This dependence is the cornerstone on which our lives are built. The recognition of our weaknesses is powerful, more powerful than any example of human strength. Such a paradox can only exist in the topsy-turvy world of Jesus Christ.

In 1978, the young coach of the St Mirren football club in Scotland was fired, as he was thought to be doing a bad job. But he would have none of it. He believed he had been dismissed unfairly and took the management to an industrial tribunal, asking to be reinstated as the club's manager.

The presiding official at the tribunal hearing rejected his claim for reinstatement and described him as "petty," "immature," and "possessing, neither by experience or talent, any managerial ability at all."[5] He set out to prove them wrong. That man was Sir Alex Ferguson, the best football manager of his generation. Pity he had to show his talents through Manchester United. Imagine if it had been Chelsea!

Jesus told us directly to *speak* to the mountain: "Truly I tell you, if anyone says to this mountain, 'Go, throw yourself into the sea,' and does not doubt in their heart but believes that what they say will happen, it will be done for them" (Mark 11:23).

This is, of course, a figure of speech. But it is an important lesson nonetheless. We should "speak to the mountain"—speak the promises of God aloud when encountering overwhelming opposition. Words of faith will dissolve the mountains of attack, destruction, and despair and wash them away, as if a mountain suddenly slid into the sea. There is something unbelievably powerful in articulating and speaking out the words of God.

Many are the times over the last forty years when I have proclaimed loudly, "I can do all things through him who strengthens me" (Philippians 4:13 ESV). And "all things" means everything necessary to fulfill God's calling for my life.

5. DON'T QUIT TOO SOON

Most of us are in danger of quitting too soon. But it is worth saying that there are a few delusional people who press on regardless of all the facts that show their ventures are futile. You only need to watch *The X Factor* or *The Voice* to know that no amount of perseverance will earn some of the contestants the singing careers they are so hungry for! This is when we rely on those closest to us to be brutally honest and help us grow in self-awareness.

But most of us will quit too soon. That is what separates the winners from the losers. Those who achieve much press on without holding back. They do not quit easily. And often, when every circumstance is against them, they still push through. Caldwell and Jorgeson persevered even as the skin was ripped from their fingers.

Paul knew what it was like to be overwhelmed by challenges and yet to press on. He told us,

> Three times I was beaten with rods, once I was pelted with stones, three times I was shipwrecked, I spent a night and a day in the open sea, I have been constantly on the move. I have been in danger from rivers, in danger from bandits, in danger from my fellow Jews, in danger from Gentiles; in danger in the city, in danger in the country, in danger at sea; and in danger from false believers. I have labored and toiled and have often gone without sleep; I have known hunger and thirst and have often gone without food; I have been cold and naked. (2 Corinthians 11:25–27)

And his list of challenges goes on.

Yet there is in these accounts one overriding, compelling, and driving force: the indomitable conviction of calling. In Paul's case of preaching the good news to the Gentiles, he would do it, whatever it took.

Calling without conviction is ineffectual. Conviction without calling is delusional. But calling and conviction empower us to endure.

Joshua marched around Jericho seven times before it fell (Joshua 6). How easy it would have been to give up after six! Elijah sent his servant seven times to check the sky before a tiny cloud appeared (1 Kings 18:44). What got them through the middle numbers?

I start down a path with conviction that it is the right one. I press on three times to lay hold of God's promise, but nothing seems to happen. Do I continue to press on or pull back? I wish I could give the definitive answer. But if I could, you should distrust me, because to do so would be to undermine the very nature of trust. It's precisely because we don't know that we have to trust God. We have to keep on keeping on until we hear otherwise. It might be seven times, or it might be seventy-seven times.

We should remain alert to the voices of people God has sent us. We should steep ourselves in the reading of Scripture and assess both our gut instincts and what the Spirit is telling us about whether to persevere. In the theatre of war, when an officer has to make a snap decision, it is made using the "go-no-go" formula; in an instant, the factors for and against are calculated. If two-thirds align positively, it's "go," and if not, it's "no-go." This may seem a crude calculation, but I have found it a useful tool.

MOVING ON

While the go-no-go model is useful, we all know that life cannot be lived according to percentages. There is another layer in decision making that relies on our gut instincts or intuitions—and if we are walking closely with God, we trust that this is where the Holy Spirit speaks to us.

And God does indeed speak. "The LORD said to Samuel, 'How long will you mourn for Saul, since I have rejected him as king over Israel? Fill your horn with oil and be on your way'" (1 Samuel 16:1).

We can get so downhearted by the problems we face, uncertainty of the future, comparison with the seemingly hassle-free lives of our friends, and lack of opportunities to use our talents effectively, that we lose hope.

When we are heavily burdened, it is right to acknowledge our state and ask God to minister to us in that painful place. But there comes a moment, which we must discern carefully, when we risk wallowing in the pain and discomfort.

I can recall a time when, between jobs, I became introspective and needed a word from God to jolt me out of dwelling on the past and move me on to new challenges. It was the right time to be rebuked, to be led "to the rock that is higher than I" (Psalm 61:2). The Spirit has often put this verse on my heart to force me to look up out of the near depression of navel-gazing and searching for solutions. Within no time I could see the future not as a painful uncertainty but as a dynamic challenge to be tackled with strength and vigor.

The past is the past, I sensed God saying to me. *It was once a great job that I called you to, but I have moved on and want you to move on to another path.* Similarly, Samuel had to come to terms with the fact that Saul, whom he had personally anointed as king, was no longer the anointed one. He had to face the biggest mistake of his life. It was hard, yet he moved on to seek out and anoint David. He had to leave behind the memories of his errors and press on to know the new season God was leading him into. Left to himself, he would have remained depressed. But so often there is a clear call from God to get with the program.

About twenty years ago, a group of us had a dream: we believed that London needed an international and nondenominational worship center. We identified the Battersea Power Station site as a place to build such a center, and we started praying. We got excited. We believed that this was the place. A Buddhist pagoda had just been put up in Battersea Park, and I thought that if a Buddhist pagoda could be built there, why not have a worship community on the Battersea Power Station? We dreamed up the scheme, we talked to architects, we talked to planners. We had the support of Prince Charles. We had beautiful images of what this centralized place would look like, with lots of ministries in one large worship community that could feed London. We had a talented team of people, developers, and planners. We put money together. But it was not to be.

I remember going there with Jamie Haith, who was one of our church youth leaders at the time, for one last chance to pray. Maybe

God would give us one final miracle and turn the project in our favor. We arrived at the site, but where we would normally go into the area, through a gate, someone had moved an enormous boulder sealing it off—we couldn't go in. Like the tomb of Jesus, it was sealed. How we hoped for a resurrection! There were many tears at the time. It seemed that a dream had died.

I picked up a little stone, which was lying next to that great big rock, as a reminder of that moment, and this stone has been on my desk for more than twenty years. I think of it often, and I think of that moment of intense disappointment. It is a reminder of the prayers and the perseverance and the fact that not all our planted seeds will germinate.

Creating that worship center had been my plan A—it was all I wanted. But plan B was to work with the team in my home church, helping the ministries there grow, to develop Alpha, and to plant church communities across the United Kingdom. In hindsight, that was God's plan A. It would not have been the right thing at that time to pull a high-profile set of ministries into one central place, when in fact growth has come much more rapidly to varied ministries at Holy Trinity Brompton.

A disappointment encountered is not a destiny canceled. We may not see the fruit of things that we would hope for, but just as the stone was rolled across the tomb of the crucified Jesus, there was, three days later, a different story.

PERSEVERANCE CREATES CHARACTER

We know that life does not always run smoothly. It takes time and perseverance to realize our God-given ambitions. Think back to Tommy Caldwell and Kevin Jorgeson climbing the Dawn Wall. Caldwell had been working on this unclimbed route since 2007 and experienced numerous failed attempts before finally finding success. In 2011, he spent six days working on just one of the thirty-two sections, suspended a third of the way up El Capitan in horrendous weather, only to be eventually forced into defeat. Even during the successful ascent in 2015, things did not go smoothly. On one of the most difficult sections, Kevin Jorgeson fell at the same point ten times over seven days, before he finally managed at the eleventh attempt. By this point, before he was even halfway up the wall, his fingers had been sliced open repeatedly on the razor-sharp rocks.

One of the most incredible aspects of Tommy Caldwell's story is that he completed this seemingly impossible climb with only nine fingers. When he was twenty-three, Caldwell accidently cut through his left index finger with a table saw—taking the finger off just above the knuckle. At the time, the doctors suggested he find a new career, and the climbing world mourned the apparent loss of a rising star. But Caldwell would not be undone or deterred. This monumental setback only made him more determined to achieve his goals. Reflecting on the value of adversity, Caldwell later wrote, "Through these experiences I learned that hardship is what changes us the most. It puts us in an intensely meditative state where we figure out what we really want. And it motivates us to go for those things we have always dreamed of."[6]

It's incredible to think that one of the first men to free-climb the unassailable Dawn Wall—the man who had pioneered the expedition and who is regarded by many as the greatest all-around climber in a generation—has managed to achieve that epithet while missing a finger!

Character is wrought in adversity and hardship. The Dawn Wall was never going to yield to a first, second, or even third attempt. Every slip and failure was a learning curve for Caldwell and Jorgeson. Every year of failed attempts added fuel to their fire. After slipping from the same spot for the tenth time in seven days, Kevin Jorgeson could muster an eleventh attempt only because he had acquired the character that comes with perseverance.

Few people achieve their life ambitions without persevering

against the odds. Calling and perseverance are siblings; they grow up together. Jack Ma, the founder of Alibaba, tells the story of how seventeen years ago he tried to raise $2 million to start his online retail business. He traveled from China and visited thirty investors in Silicon Valley. He was turned down by each one in turn. He was dejected and returned home. He then scraped together the money needed to start his business from friends and family. Finally he succeeded, and in 2014 Alibaba became the largest company to raise money on the New York Stock Exchange, valuing the company at $250 billion.

One of the early investors remembered meeting Jack on a visit to China to find investment opportunities. He said he met twenty entrepreneurs but invested in only one—Alibaba—because he had never seen such hunger in the eyes of one young person. Hunger to fulfill our God-given callings and perseverance remain inseparable from achievement.

Paul made this very point in his letter to the Romans, when he told the church in Rome to rejoice in their sufferings, for "suffering produces perseverance; perseverance, character; and character, hope" (Romans 5:3–4). Paul teaches us that when we press on, something meaningful is happening, even if we don't recognize it. Our characters are being formed. Character is forged in the struggle to persevere. Setbacks do not end our aspirations; they teach us to build resilience, to learn how to flourish even when the chips are down. We toughen up. We are not fazed by adversity. We learn to trust in Jesus. This is an integral part of the way the Spirit of God increases the tenacity within us. Resilience enables us to grow into the people we would like to be when no one is watching.

CELEBRATE THE END

Finally, and gloriously, we celebrate because our plans are completed. In the story of Zechariah, there was a paean of praise because the work was done: "What are you, mighty mountain? Before Zerubbabel you will become level ground. Then he will bring out the capstone to shouts of 'God bless it! God bless it!'" (Zechariah 4:7). This verse rings with the sound of grace. The stone was taken from the quarry where it had been excavated, chiseled, and refined. His hands laid this capstone, the crucial part of the building, and they would also complete it. And then the people would know that God had been in the project. "The hands of Zerubbabel have laid the foundation of this temple; his hands will also complete it. Then you will know that the LORD Almighty has sent me to you" (v. 9).

There comes a time when, after the quarrying and chiseling and refining, we show the completed product. After a time of trial there is a time of grace in which we achieve what we have been called to do. Perhaps someone's life has changed from being self-driven to being Spirit-led, or a new task at work is finished against the odds, or a manuscript is accepted for publication after the seventh rejection, or a challenge has been completed on the eleventh attempt. Whatever it is, it is time to celebrate, to rejoice, and to look back and see the hand of God guiding you through the trials.

Reuben Morgan and Ben Fielding of Hillsong have written one of the most awe-inspiring songs of our time, "Mighty to Save." It has been sung millions of times all over the world. There is a line in the song that has become a refrain to many throughout the world—the declaration that our Savior can move the mountains.[7]

Over and over again, in times of praying with people, I have come back to claiming this promise with them. I remember one occasion sitting in church next to a distressed man who was a foreign exchange trader. He had dabbled with a number of things that were clearly unhelpful, from pornography to semioccult activities. It was by chance that we happened to be sitting next to each other, but hindsight tells me it was another instance of God working all things for good. As the worship grew, I sensed this man's continuing distress until I eventually plucked up the courage to ask whether there was anything I could do to help. He looked at me as if to say there was nothing that could be done. "My life is a mess," he said. "I have big issues. I sense darkness within me." I took him into a side chapel where we could be alone, and we began to pray. At exactly the same time the worship team, led by Tim Hughes, was singing "Mighty to Save." It was new to me then. But I knew in an instant that there was great power in the words and the music.

As they sang about the Savior who can move mountains, I encouraged my friend to speak directly, in the name of Jesus, to each of the "mountains" he was confronting. It was an alarming experience. He became contorted and physically sick (fortunately the door was close by!). We prayed on with determination. And slowly but unmistakably, these strongholds of despair that had been there all his life, deep-seated like a mountain, began to move. We recognized in that moment the power of worship to unlock the power of God to move mountains of shame, oppression, and guilt.

This man was clearly under an attack, an attempt to destabilize his life. But the power of God was upon him. Freedom came to him. Even now, years later, I can still see the color come back in his face and the peace surrounding him. He never looked back. Those mountains had been truly moved and thrown into the sea. For him it happened in an instant; for others (such as me) obstacles take longer to be dislodged. I wish it were not so.

A South African friend once said to me, "You must not say, 'God, I have a big problem,' but, 'Problem, I have a big God.'" Simple but true. And sometimes our God takes his time in removing those mountains, as he teaches us about his faithfulness, tests our trust in him, and edifies our characters. In all cases, however, our God will flatten the mountains that are opposed to his ways in our lives. Only his time will tell when and how.

NINE

CALLED TO WORSHIP

WORSHIP LIFTS OUR EYES TO ADORE THE CREATOR. IN WORship we seek the presence of God. In his presence there is perfect peace. As such, worship is not just a momentary impulse or a feel-good expression of gratitude for a happy day. It is more. It is the architecture of life: the constant reminder that we are enjoying the favor of God. When fears threaten to overwhelm us, worship reminds us of this favor. Our callings make no sense outside of worship, because worship acknowledges that calling as coming from, inspired by, and sustained by God himself. We buy in to a plan bigger than our own. His purposes are "for welfare and not for evil"; his plans give us "a future and a hope" (Jeremiah 29:11 ESV). Therefore, the search for our callings needs to take place within the search for intimacy with God. It is only from a relational perspective that we will be able to discern his plans for our lives.

Of all the rituals and traditions of the Christian faith, singing songs of worship to God can seem most peculiar. Can it really happen in the real world? It feels so surreal. I was talking to a friend of mine some time ago who simply didn't understand worship. "Is it just about singing or is there more? Does worship have any relevance to my everyday life? Why are these songs so important to God? Does God somehow need the constant praise and affirmation?"

The answer, of course, is no. God does not need our worship

or praise. He is complete in and of himself—he has no needs or requirements. And yet worship forms an integral part of our faith. Many of the major figures in the Bible sang songs of praise not only in times of victory but also in the valleys of despair. Worship is for all seasons of life. The book of Psalms is full of songs of worship. Paul wrote to the early church of the importance of singing "psalms and hymns and spiritual songs . . . to the Lord" (Ephesians 5:19 ESV). The book of Revelation speaks of four creatures who worship God day after day and night after night (Revelation 4:8), and it looks forward to a time when all creatures in heaven and on earth will praise the Lamb (Revelation 5:13).

Clearly, we are called to worship God. But why does it matter if we give praise and glory to God? And what does worship have to do with our wider callings to engage with the world?

It's important to point out that worship is not confined to music. After all, we can't go around singing songs all day unless we are a little unstable. Rather, *worship* is a broad term describing any display of surrender, praise, and submission to the name who is above all other names, Jesus Christ.

Far from being limited to singing songs on a Sunday, worship is the lifting of all that we are to God—in song, but also in prayer, in the natural world, in meditation, at work, in creativity, and with humble and reverent adoration. Worship should be apparent at all times, not just at church on Sundays. The supreme objective of our worship is to be drawn into the presence of the living God. We become parched and thirsty during our ordinary routines. We worship God to refresh ourselves and, above all, to encounter him.

I've said regularly that my workstation is my worship station. Our careers should praise and glorify God. It means working well at our callings, having moments of quiet prayer and reflection throughout the day. Some might put on headphones and listen to a worship album while they work. But worship is also expressed through outward acts of love. Perhaps worshipping at work means giving glory to God through acts of service, even if it's just washing up everyone else's mugs in the office kitchen in addition to doing our jobs to the best of our God-given abilities. It means performing our day-to-day work with honesty and integrity, not to gain the praise of our superiors, but to honor God in everything we do. Such offerings are a powerful way of worshipping, and they help shape our hearts to be more like that of Christ. In worship we acknowledge that he is sovereign over every part of our lives; we take time to worship to affirm our complete dependence on him. Through worship we lay down even our callings to ensure that we remain submissive to his will.

Worship can be done collectively, but it can also be done alone. We experience a great sense of celebration when singing with like-minded people. Joining with other Christians at work, as a small worshipping community within the workplace, can be powerful and rewarding.

But times alone—drawing close to God in silence, in meditation, or through reading scriptures or biblical commentaries—are also powerful.

So we should not allow worship to be trapped in the guitar case of contemporary music. It has a far wider, richer source that resonates, deep unto deep (Psalm 42:7), into every aspect of our lives, in different ways to different people.

I don't want to play down the importance of worship expressed through song. It is an incredibly important way of praising God and has been done by Christians across the world for two millennia. It remains central to Christian communities' corporate expression of love, adoration, and thankfulness to their Creator and Redeemer.

Sung worship has been particularly important for me throughout my Christian life. I frequently have a line from a song running through my head during the day. Tim Hughes's "The Cross Stands" is a reminder of the victory of Christ, and Matt Redman's "Through It All" ministers to me when the stress of life hits really hard.

Alongside bands like Hillsong United, Bethel, and Soul Survivor, these worship leaders have shaped a generation's attitude to worship.

I am often asked why modern worship has had such a profound effect on young people globally. There are, of course, many reasons, but I am always particularly struck by the way in which the lyrics of many contemporary worship songs reach untapped longings in the younger generation's hearts, connecting with the zeitgeist of the age in a profound way. The words capture their yearnings for something deeper. This generation that has grown up with quick fixes, with knowledge just a Google search away, with relationships that are rarely more than skin deep. So many are searching for depth—something that gives a sense of purpose and belonging. And this is what worship is able to offer. It helps put into words and music something we might otherwise struggle to express.

WORSHIP AS RESPONSE

When we recognize who God is and what he has done for us, it is only natural to respond in praise and adoration. This is the God who created the heavens and the earth, who flung stars into space, and yet who loves us, cares for us, and has redeemed us with the death of Jesus on the cross. He is the one who calls us into his service.

In his grace God has given us a way of responding to his love and majesty through worship. Worship enables us to give something back to God. Not something he needs, not something that could ever do justice to his majesty and glory, but something that he accepts, as a loving father might accept the colorful scribbling of a child. If God refused our worship, then relationship with him would be impossible. True relationship must be two-sided, not one-way.

When my children were growing up, they listened to story tapes (those were the days!). In one of them, a character would express great joy by saying that something was "absolutely wonderfully marvelous." For no particular reason, it stuck, as silly phrases often do, and is now a recurrent refrain in the family whenever something is amazing and cannot adequately be described in words.

The purpose of worship is to marvel at the amazing nature of God and his goodness. As Psalm 8:1 puts it:

> LORD, our Lord,
>> how majestic is your name in all the earth!
>
> You have set your glory
>> in the heavens.

Today, we marvel too little. Standing awestruck in the presence of God is a rare, precious, life-giving experience. Many of us find his presence through a sense of the wonder at the natural world, whether standing at the top of a mountain, experiencing the power of a thunderstorm, or simply admiring the color of lavender or the fragility of a butterfly's wings. But in our busy, stressed lives, there is simply not enough time to marvel, to be astonished by and enjoy the presence of God, to be in his presence for no other reason than that we long to be there waiting on him.

And the aliveness of his presence is true not just on Sundays. God is not contained within the walls of church or the worship set. His presence goes with us and is active, even though we might feel it less at work. We need to find a way to marvel at his goodness both in the Sunday service and also while we are trying, often with difficulty, to align our wills with his desires.

Worship isn't, however, only for the good times; it is for the bad times as well. It is for *all* times. David knew how to praise God during all seasons: when depressed (Psalm 42), when rejoicing (Psalm 32), when needing guidance (Psalm 25). And it is true that God is enthroned on the praises of his people (Psalm 22:3) or "leaning back on the cushions of Israel's praise" as *The Message* puts it.

Once I was truly overwhelmed by the stress of getting a piece of work done. I remember thinking I needed to refocus and reestablish priorities. I knew I could not do it alone, and I also knew that the key to unlocking the situation lay in worship. I made a choice to recognize God's goodness and power rather than to slip into unhelpful default responses. I telephoned a friend who is a worship leader, and we agreed to meet that evening. He started playing his guitar and pouring out his songs of worship. I simply allowed the presence of God to grow in intensity. The music surrounded us, as if the angels of the Lord were there too. A distinctive presence of the Spirit of God hovered over us. As time went on, a change came over me, and I sensed the deep quietening of the Spirit and the beginnings of the peace that passes all understanding. After an hour or so of sung worship—gentle, engaging, and intentional—I began to receive the confidence that I needed to complete what I had been called to do. And, feeling I was transformed through worship, I was able—even within a deeply stressful situation—to marvel at God's power and goodness and love for me.

In *The Rime of the Ancient Mariner*, the poet Samuel Taylor Coleridge painted a vivid picture of what happens when we praise God. The albatross that has been following the ship has been shot dead, and the mariner is now under an unbreakable curse. Parched and alone, in the middle of a dead sea, he tries to pray to God for salvation but cannot muster the strength. Then he notices the beauty of the ocean and the creatures around his ship, and from somewhere deep within him, he starts to praise God for the beauty of creation.

> O happy living things! no tongue
> Their beauty might declare:
> A spring of love gush'd from my heart,
> And I bless'd them unaware . . .
> The selfsame moment I could pray;
> And from my neck so free
> The Albatross fell off, and sank
> Like lead into the sea.[1]

Suddenly, the curse is broken. The rains come and the winds blow, and he is finally able to make for land. But it was only when he lifted his eyes to God that the dramatic change occurred. It was only when he stopped thinking about his own situation that he was able to transcend it.

Praise forces us to lift our heads, to look up. We don't praise with our heads down. It is a powerful offensive weapon. When the armies of Moab and Ammon marched against King Jehoshaphat and Judah, the king responded by placing worshippers at the front of his army. They led the march crying out, "Give thanks to the LORD, for his love endures forever" (2 Chronicles 20:21). As they transcended their immediate peril, God protected Judah without them ever having to draw a sword. With their eyes fixed on the glory of God, and their hearts giving praise to his name, God defended them from the threat of invasion.

Revelation 18 offers a chilling warning about a world that refuses to acknowledge God. Babylon is a metaphor for commercial life lived without God and directed toward only unjust gain: "The fruit you longed for is gone from you. All your luxury and splendor have vanished, never to be recovered" (v. 14). Worship is nonexistent: "The music of harpists and musicians, pipers and trumpeters, will never be heard in you again" (v. 22). Indeed, "in one hour [Babylon] has been brought to ruin!" (v. 19). Neither trade nor worship is found in this barren place: "The light of a lamp will never shine in you again" (v. 23).

The cries of jubilation in heaven at the fall of Babylon are deafening: "Hallelujah! Salvation and glory and power belong to our God, for true and just are his judgments" (Revelation 19:1–2).

Many run after luxuries and splendor, of course. They can be so tempting. They draw us in and tie us up. They cancel worship. They pervert our callings. Yet worship unites us, rebalances us, and reminds us to tie ourselves first to God—to seek first his kingdom. Worship emphasizes that we are not made for this life only—but for eternity. Worship is our daily affirmation of our divine aspirations.

And it can be a daily conflagration of idols that threaten to destroy us: a bonfire of the vanities, experienced not in some future judgment but today.

My life would become a desert if it were not refreshed in worship by the living waters of his Spirit. To give glory and honor to God each day in all that I am called to do is the supreme calling on my life. It is what I wholeheartedly desire, above all other things—to offer myself as "a living sacrifice, holy and pleasing to God." This, according to Paul, is "true and proper worship" (Romans 12:1).

WORSHIP AS REALIGNMENT

The primary purpose of worship is to glorify and honor God on account of who he is and as a response to the untold riches of his mercy. But that is not its only effect. Worship looks to God, but it has a profound effect on us, strengthening and confirming our particular callings.

Psalm 95 gives us great perspective on the central importance of worship:

> Come, let us bow down in worship,
>> let us kneel before the LORD our Maker;
> for he is our God
>> and we are the people of his pasture,
>> the flock under his care. (vv. 6–7)

In this statement of worship, the psalmist is reminded of his own place in the grand scheme of creation. This God we worship is *our* God. We are under his care and his guidance. Worship is therefore a reminder of our priorities, of our callings, and of our place in the created order. One of the effects of engaging in worship is to realign ourselves with the one who is the source of life and light.

It is a constant struggle to have our wills bent to his. Our protective human shells need to be penetrated by the breaking in of God's presence to bring about a reordering of our self-driven lives. This reorientation is vital to keep our callings on the rails. Worship is the way we keep open and fresh in our relationships with God. It is a simple truth: shape or be shaped. Let worship shape your life—or be shaped by the world.

The act of singing often makes us vulnerable and more ready to connect to God with our emotions, in the same way that Shakespeare turned to poetry when writing about love and grief but returned to prose when dealing with the everyday.

Recently, I was speaking to a men's group on the importance of daily worship. It is a myth that men don't enjoy worshipping together, that it is too emotional. I have seen the effects of worship on the most hardened of men. There is within all of us a craving for intimacy as we come before God.

Before iron ore can be shaped, it must be made malleable through the intense heat of a smelting furnace. We need to be prepared to be bent into shape during worship, but before we are bent into shape, we must be willing to be bent out of shape. The ore is totally out of shape when being prepared in the smelting furnace to be poured out. And so for us, in the fire of worship, we allow the Holy Spirit to work within us to change our hardened hearts and minds.

There is, therefore, something quite robust about the call to worship. It is not an insipid lulling of the emotions by pretty songs; it is at times fiercely uncomfortable. Worship is not just soothing background mood music; it is awe-inspiring, provocative, and urgent, challenging us out of our comfort zones to reflect, realize, and realign our callings.

There is a moment of spiritual maturity when we realize that God is able to speak to us and shape us in all times of worship—whether we are singing together at a Christian gathering, listening to songs on our own, walking along savoring the presence of God in prayer, or working at our jobs.

As we become vulnerable to God in worship, we become malleable to him—open to the work of his transformative power. This is so important if we are to align our priorities and desires with his.

The Bible makes it clear that worship is not uncontested by other "gods." We have a choice to worship the God revealed to us in the Bible or the other gods of money, power, sex, and success. Worship is not neutral territory. There is a competition for our hearts and minds. This is why David affirmed that he would praise God above all other gods: "For you, LORD, are the Most High over all the earth; you are exalted far above all gods" (Psalm 97:9). There is a direct calling to us to choose which god we will worship. The idols of today might not be made of wood or carved images, but they have just as powerful a pull on us.

Satan loves to see us confuse our priorities. He loves to see us chase after other idols. What God underwrites, the devil undermines. That's his way in the world. We are told to be vigilant, as the devil's efforts to unsettle our trust in God are compared to that of a lion going about trying to devour his prey: "Your enemy the devil prowls around like a roaring lion looking for someone to devour" (1 Peter 5:8).

Anyone who has seen a lion going after prey in the wilds of Africa will recognize the dramatic power of this image. I remember watching a lion move within inches of our tent while on safari in Africa. He was merely walking by, not seeking to attack us, but that was scary enough. The deep, resonant growling made us hold our breaths. One false move or sound and we would be mauled. Only God and my dry cleaner know how scared I was!

A lion in full chase is as chilling and brutal a sight as one could ever hope to see. We therefore remain on guard against the devil, as anyone on safari in Africa would be if they were walking in an area where there were clear lion tracks. I assure you that your eyes and ears are open and alert to any noise.

The act of worship, therefore, is a constant reminder of who holds the call on our lives, our time, our resources, and our energy. When we choose to worship God, we are recognizing the God to whom we bow down. No other god has a claim on us. That is what David is celebrating in Psalm 95.

It is worth remembering that however powerful a lion can be, he can be driven away when a herd of buffalo come together to see him off. He can pick them off individually, but collectively they drive him away. There is power in the name of Jesus and even greater power when we come together to thwart the devil's attacks. When we join in collective worship, we are to protect not only our own hearts but also those of our brothers and sisters in Christ.

When the devil set about undermining Adam and Eve, he did so with a crafty use of the question "Did God really say, 'You must not eat from any tree in the garden'?" (Genesis 3:1). Of course, it was the opposite of what God had commanded: "You are free to eat from any tree in the garden; but you must not eat from the tree of the knowledge of good and evil, for when you eat from it you will certainly die" (Genesis 2:16–17). The devil will always try to make our freedom seem like bondage. And he does so with a condescending tone of voice. This is his tactic—not a full-frontal assault but a slithering alongside, trying to cast doubt on God's way in our lives. You might hear the words in your mind, *Are you* really *up to it?* Or, *Was your father not right when he said you were no good at anything?* We need to beware his cunning and resist his efforts to twist God's Word.

When we worship, we keep sight of the fact that "the one who is in [us] is greater than the one who is in the world" (1 John 4:4). Christ has the victory, and we need to constantly remember this is not a war between two equal forces, although at times it might appear to be so. The war has been won, but the struggles and the skirmishes to prevent us from fulfilling our callings will continue until the final day. Worship gives us the energy to hold tight to God and to our callings.

When we worship, we engage in warfare. We declare the will of God: "your will be done on earth as it is in heaven" (Matthew 6:10). And we have the victory! The powers of evil will not overcome us or deflect us from his purposes. The whole of the book of Acts was written with one overriding theme: the will of God cannot be thwarted by the powers of evil. In worship, we are anointed by the Spirit of God to combat every effort to unsettle us from fulfilling that call of God in our lives.

Let us be ready and prepared to stand firm:

> Therefore put on the full armor of God, so that when the day of evil comes, you may be able to stand your ground, and after you have done everything, to stand. Stand firm then, with the belt of truth buckled around your waist, with the breastplate of righteousness in place, and with your feet fitted with the readiness that comes from the gospel of peace. In addition to all this, take up the shield of faith, with which you can extinguish all the flaming arrows of the evil one. Take the helmet of salvation and the sword of the Spirit, which is the word of God. (Ephesians 6:13–17)

Worship, then, equips us for the battle ahead. It is a time of preparation and training. I have a friend who was in the Special Air Service, the front line of covert military operations. An essential part of his training was the repeated command, "Check your exit." This must become an unconscious habit: even when parking a car, one makes sure that it's pointing the right way to get out. Exit from danger matters. And worship is the best way I know to get away from the dangers of distraction, fear, and repeated sins.

Worship is the child's longing to be with the Father, who pours out love, encouragement, and guidance. It is the child's pleasure in spending time with a devoted parent, receiving boundless support and kindness. No calling can be sustained without the constant encouragement and affirmation that comes from God through worship.

WORSHIP AS RECEIVING

Realignment is not the only effect of worship. We are shaped, but we are also equipped. Although it is an outpouring of our praise to God, worship becomes a time when we receive from God. Worship opens us to intimate interaction with him. As we interact, so we receive the empowering and life-transforming presence of the Holy Spirit.

When we receive the presence of God, we become the presence of God in the world—wherever we are called to be. There is something deeply alluring about the presence of Christ. It changes the atmosphere. Worship gives us the "aroma of Christ" (2 Corinthians 2:15)—and others pick it up. But it doesn't just attract others; it changes us.

Worship is the way in which I remove myself as the center of the universe and return this incarnate, reconciling God to that place. We will always struggle to allow the center of gravity to shift from ourselves to God. That is what happened at the fall: we tried to make ourselves into gods. But now, in Christ and by his Spirit, God enables us to love him and to give our lives in service for others.

Paul set out a key calling to all Christians—to become a new creation: "The old has passed away; behold, the new has come" (2 Corinthians 5:17 ESV). And part of this newness is a call to be reconcilers of the world to God, just as Christ reconciled the world through himself. This is a passage of immense power. Grasp this message, and your life will never be the same again. Why so? One of the key thoughts in the works of Karl Barth, perhaps the greatest theologian of the twentieth century, is that alienation was the basic dysfunction of humanity.[2] The true calling of all Christians is to be the ones who, in Christ, become the reconcilers of humanity, just as God, in Christ, reconciled the world.

Every day we see this alienation of humanity working itself out. We have estranged relationships in our families, tension at work, disagreements with colleagues on contracts or negotiations, disputes between people, political animosity, and political antipathies between nations. The list of dysfunctional behavior goes on, and our task is to bring the good news of reconciliation to each of these fractious situations. Christ makes his reconciling appeal through us, and we become involved in this drawing together and reconciling of all those many situations where people are divided.

Our workplaces are no different. They reflect the tensions of living alienated from God. And we are the ones who have the privilege, in the contact we have with people around us, to be his spokespeople for conflict resolution. It is fundamental to all callings. In worship we gain the strength and the motivation to continue being the ones who help patch things up, untangle the knots of prejudice, and counter the negative self-images that people are forced into. In these ways, we who are changed through worship collectively can change the world.

To carry the presence of Christ is a huge privilege, and often it seems confined to people of such obviously saintly qualities as to make most of us feel marginalized. "I am no Mother Teresa," a friend told me knowingly. Of that fact I was well aware. Several parts of his life were not running smoothly together. But he wanted to be recognized as a person who carried the presence of God with him.

Tattoos almost always tell a story. Often, they commemorate something meaningful, and a person with a tattoo wants to be able to show it off. Saint Paul wrote, "I bear on my body the marks of Jesus" (Galatians 6:17). Figuratively, he carries Christ's tattoos, and they are there for all to see—a living memory. We, too, carry Christ's presence in the world today as if it were a tat.

The more we worship him, the more Christlike we become. And it was Christ who "did not consider equality with God something to be used to his own advantage; rather, he made himself nothing by taking the very nature of a servant" (Philippians 2:6–7). He made humility his hallmark. If we are to carry his presence, the tattoo we bear will be humility.

WORSHIP AND CALLING

Worship is ultimately the key to our callings: the place where much of what is hidden from our understanding is unlocked. Worship is the place where we receive wisdom and revelation, where our eyes are enlightened to know the hope to which God has called us (Ephesians 1:17–18). It opens our hearts and minds to new possibilities and fresh challenges. It quickens our conscience. It is thus where our callings start, are strengthened, and are sustained. We cannot stay the course of our callings without it. It is both the entry point into a new way of living for God and an exit from the encircling pressures of life around us, which can draw us away from or dilute our first love of God.

The Holy Spirit leads us into worship as the ultimate goal of our lives. Worship is a whole-of-life experience and an attitude of the heart. It is the alignment of our hopes and desires with those God has for us. The more aligned our wills are with his will, the more effective our lives become. The more intimate we are prepared to be, the more we will find worship opening up our closed lives. In worship, we lay down our crowns and ambitions, we escape our self-centeredness and self-indulgences, and we find our perspectives restored in the light of his love.

Worship is to calling what the air is to breathing: life-giving, essential, impossible to survive without. Without worship the experienced life of Christ is dormant within us, and his Spirit is grieved.

True worship celebrates our callings. We are drawn into the greatest privilege for a human being: to worship the living God. The book of Revelation ends with the invitation, "Let the one who is thirsty come; and let the one who wishes take the free gift of the water of life" (Revelation 22:17). This is what sustains, refreshes, nourishes, and strengthens us—this water of life, the only true elixir that will give us eternal worshipping life.

Worship is the most important thing I can do on this earth.

The great opening sentence of the Bible—"In the beginning God . . ." (Genesis 1:1)—captures this starting point for all worship. It was his initiative. I could not worship him unless he had first put that desire into my heart by allowing his Son to change my life. It is a fundamental tenet of my life that trust in Jesus Christ changes everything. And the exciting part is that worship is the way in which, through this extraordinary two-way street of encounter, we are able to commune with God himself. What greater calling could there be on our lives?

But perhaps the greatest truth is that we can worship him wherever we are. We do not need to go to some special place. The Samaritan woman who met Jesus at the well (John 4) was told that no longer would believers have to worship in a particular place—Jerusalem—or in a particular way, or at a particular time. Instead we would worship "in the Spirit and in truth" (v. 24). A whole new world opened up. We can meet God anywhere at any time, enabled by his Spirit, even at work! But who is this Spirit who is the power behind the call to worship?

TEN

CALLED TO BREAK BORDERS

*Dear, dear Corinthians, I can't tell you how much I long for you
to enter this wide-open, spacious life. We didn't fence you in. The
smallness you feel comes from within you. Your lives aren't small,
but you're living them in a small way. I'm speaking as plainly as I
can and with great affection. Open up your lives. Live openly and
expansively!*

—2 CORINTHIANS 6:11–13 THE MESSAGE

SINCE MY FAITH IN JESUS CHRIST CAME ALIVE, I HAVE LONGED
to experience more of the presence of the empowering Spirit as I
work out my calling—often, as the Scriptures indicate, "with fear
and trembling" (Philippians 2:12). Perhaps you come at it another
way. You long to put into effect the calling you sense there is on your
life, but you lack the power, the energy, or the inclination to do so.
So often we think that only other people have callings. There have
been times when the calling on my life is strong and I feel confident
and ready to attack the world; then there are those seasons when my
calling is cold and confidence is low.

How do we keep our callings in good repair so that they grow
into a flame and don't just flicker?

The answer for us, as it was for those first disciples at the beginning of Acts, is the Holy Spirit.

Why? Because we cannot do it without him. His greatest task
is to make our callings known to us and to confirm them along the

way. We simply cannot flourish in our God-given callings without the daily in-filling of the Holy Spirit. We are temples of the Holy Spirit (1 Corinthians 3:16); our very bodies are where he dwells. When he flows, we flourish. He is the unbroken and unchanging current that courses from creation through Christ to us, helping us to be the people who we really long to be. He is the flow of our lives, the currency of the kingdom. Did you know that the words *current* and *currency* derive from the same Latin root meaning "fluidity"? As currency enables an economy to function, so the Spirit facilitates the economy of the kingdom of God.

Whether through worship, prayer, Scripture reading, or meditation, we need to renew our connection with the Spirit each day. True fullness of life is impossible without him, while life with him knows no end of possibility. Therefore we are told to "be filled with the Spirit" (Ephesians 5:18). We are constantly in need of his power.

He enables us to break through the borders of self-limitation, and every day he challenges us afresh to live risky lives for Christ. Our lives become enriched, challenged, and changed. The kingdom grows because we are prepared to take up our callings, which change not only our lives but the lives of those around us.

That Christ died and rose again two thousand years ago is of great assurance to me. That he will come again at the end of time and initiate a new heaven and a new earth I have no doubt. But what matters to me is *now*. The past and the future are persuasive, but the present is compelling. The Holy Spirit reminds us of the events of Christ's life in the past and of the promise of the full restoration of creation in the future. Above all, he reminds us how to live life to the full in the here and now. That's why he is key to life.

WHO NEEDS THE HOLY SPIRIT?

There is a view that the Holy Spirit is given to those who are especially saintly: the pope, perhaps, or Mother Teresa, or the archbishop of Canterbury. Wherever this view has come from, it is certainly not from the New Testament. Jesus makes it clear that the Holy Spirit will be given to all: "how much more will your Father in heaven give the Holy Spirit to those who ask him!" (Luke 11:13). Jesus makes it clear that each person who asks receives. Asking is the only test; there is no other qualification for receiving the Spirit. Receiving is the great promise.

James, a youth leader, once came to talk to me about the lack of direction in his life. He had no sense of calling. "Have you prayed to be filled with the Spirit?" I asked. He gave the sort of vague answer that clearly indicated that he didn't really believe that the Spirit had much to do with his day-to-day life, being instead active only in times of worship and on Sundays. It was a memorable time of prayer as he opened himself for the first time to receive the fullness of the Spirit's power in every area of his life.

In Acts 1–2, a group of people huddled together in the Upper Room. On the face of it, they could not have been more devoted to Jesus. They were, however, depressed. Their leader had died on a cross. He had returned, but then he left them again. They couldn't understand. Their calling to see a new kingdom come was seemingly at an end, and the future looked bleak. But the following day, at Pentecost, a mighty rushing wind blew them away, tongues of fire descended upon the whole gathering, and they were filled with the Holy Spirit.

We can see ourselves in one or more of these characters who were present at that depressing wake in the Upper Room: doubting Thomas; Simon the hothead; John, Jesus' closest disciple; Peter, the chosen leader who was desperate to please but became Christ's denier; Andrew, who responded so rapidly to the first call of Christ; Matthew, the tax collector who must have been ostracized by the community; Matthias, the new kid on the block who had only just been elected an apostle the day before; not to mention Joseph, a.k.a. Justus, who lost out in the election as successor to Judas. And Mary, who had been filled with the Spirit when the angel Gabriel appeared to her more than thirty years before. She was there. Why ever did she need to be filled with the Spirit again? Here they were together, along with other women and Jesus' brothers. All had different temperaments, backgrounds, and spiritual conditions; all needed the Spirit to enable them to make the most of the rest of their lives. Far from their callings ending along with Jesus' life on earth, the Spirit came visibly to reignite them.

Without the Spirit, they would have been dejected followers of a failed Messiah. The Acts of the Apostles is the continuation of the story of Christ. The last act of Jesus is the beginning of a new story that continues today and will continue until Christ comes again. As Jesus said to the disciples, "Unless I go away, the Advocate will not come to you; but if I go, I will send him to you" (John 16:7). Our understanding of the Gospels is incomplete unless we have read the book of Acts. In the same way, our callings are incomplete unless we acknowledge and embrace the Spirit of God.

The Spirit of God changed the disciples' lives—and the world. That group grasped their callings with vigor, turned the world upside down, and changed the course of history. A new boldness seized them as they realized that they were part of the greatest calling on earth, and the world has never been the same since.

This is our moment. We are not just given some vague sense of destiny and left to work it out by ourselves. But through the infilling of the Spirit given to each of us, we are taken each day, from where we are and whatever personality type we are, to the next step of the revelation of Christ for our lives. We begin to show the fruit of the Spirit—"love, joy, peace, forbearance, kindness, goodness, faithfulness, gentleness and self-control" (Galatians 5:22–23)—for no calling is valid if it does not make us more like Christ.

THE SPIRIT BREAKS BORDERS

In 1770, a fourteen-year-old boy visited the Sistine Chapel to hear the singing of the *Miserere*, a meditation on Psalm 51 by Allegri, the sixteenth-century composer. The Vatican at the time did not allow the reproduction of the music for use outside the Sistine Chapel. Anyone who flouted the prohibition was to be excommunicated. The music remained the preserve of an elite until that fourteen-year-old boy heard it. He left the Sistine Chapel and transcribed the work flawlessly from memory. That boy was Mozart. And from that moment, the *Miserere* could be performed everywhere. It was released to the world and was soon performed all over Europe.

It is now performed regularly worldwide, especially at the start of Lent. I first heard the *Miserere* on Ash Wednesday in King's College Chapel in Cambridge. To this day, I remember the effect of this deeply moving reflection on the most famous penitential psalm. I thought of David, desperate for God's forgiveness, and I thought of the need for my own life to straighten out. The music has a haunting solo part for a young treble that reaches to the depths of the soul.

What was bound into one place for a particular purpose for an elite group was disseminated far and wide and made accessible to all. That is what the Spirit does. He took what was confined to a particular time and place in Palestine and broke geographical, cultural, and religious borders so the risen Jesus would be accessible to all. But even more than that, the Spirit is the one who is constantly by our side reminding us of our callings, giving us insight into our work, and equipping us for each task.

When I was in South Africa with Joel Houston and Hillsong United at the start of their Zion Tour, I sat with some friends for the sold-out evening worship event. It was extraordinarily moving. My eyes clouded over with memories. Around me, with hands lifted high, were thousands of people of every race and age, worshipping together. I remembered the times when, as a student in South Africa during the apartheid years, meetings were racially segregated, and the law prohibited contact between people of different ethnic groups. Now I was at a Christian worship event and around me the "rainbow nation," so called by Archbishop Tutu, was shining. I choked back the tears, eventually giving in. It was deeply moving, and I was stirred to the depths of my spirit by the sight of thousands of worshippers drawn together from every cultural and racial background, praising Jesus in the capital city, Pretoria, which had been the bastion of racial oppression in the apartheid years.

As I listened through the tears, a young Australian singer, Taya Smith, sang a song, "Oceans," from Hillsong's new album. The chorus tells of the work of the Spirit breaking borders, smashing barriers, and crossing divides.[1] The words leapt at me. It was the song's first major outing internationally, and I had not heard it before. I knew in an instant that it was a truly anointed song for our time. Not only is it a Spirit-inspired song, but seeing the borders erected by the apartheid regime now destroyed all around me made it an even more powerful and prophetic experience.

I cannot forget that evening. After the event, while traveling back in the car, I told one of the band members about the painful memories of those days and the healing I'd received from that song. He listened, tears flowed, and we prayed. It is vivid to me even now as I write. I believe that "Oceans" will continue to have a profound and healing effect wherever it is sung.

At the same time, the news broadcasts were telling us of the activities of a French charity, Médecins Sans Frontières, which operates without borders in the world. Their clear calling was to meet medical needs wherever they occurred. The spokesperson was reporting on their work in Syria for people caught up on both sides of the civil war. He explained that there are no frontiers to human need, and the charity workers are where the needs are. These are truly works of the Spirit of God. His grace knows no borders when it comes to meeting the needs of humanity.

We see in the book of Acts that the Spirit of God breaks down people's preconceptions and prejudices, their limitations and assumptions about what is or is not possible. The Spirit of God is here to break down borders, and he gives us the power to roam freely across them. The ultimate human borders of sin and death do not hold. The Spirit is at work, breaking every obstacle to living out our callings in the world.

NEW LIFE

All of us have preconceptions of how God should work in our lives. We need the Spirit to show us how these assumptions might not be the true understanding of his ways. In Acts 1, the last question the disciples asked of the risen Lord before his ascension was, "Will you at this time restore the kingdom to Israel?" (v. 6 ESV). In other words, "When are we going to have executive authority so we can throw the Romans out?"

In that one sentence, they showed that they misunderstood Jesus' mission of the three previous years. They still longed for a new regime: they wanted to define a group of people living in a finite geographical area and sharing a particular privilege. They fixated on their expectations of a political regime change. They had not grasped the message of grace, which transcends borders.

Then, in the powerful response, the paradigm was broken. Their model was one of an enclosed group, but Jesus replied, "You will receive power when the Holy Spirit comes on you" (v. 8). He now comes to establish a new dynamic in which his power is not restricted to one people but can be given to all people. Jesus continued, "and you will be my witnesses in Jerusalem, and in all Judea and Samaria, and *to the ends of the earth*" (v. 8, emphasis added). He could not have made it clearer that there are no limits to the power and the reach of God in heaven to the peoples of earth.

Perhaps the most moving account of a barrier being broken is the exchange between Peter and Cornelius in Acts 10. We need to read this seminal exchange with the same openness to the Spirit that Peter had. There will be the same challenges in our time as there were for Peter.

Peter saw a vision filled with every imaginable unclean, non-kosher animal, which must have been anathema to every instinct he had. He heard a voice saying, "Get up, Peter. Kill and eat" (v. 13). He resisted and was rebuked with the words, "Do not call anything impure that God has made clean" (v. 15). This happened three times, and then the vision disappeared. Peter, despite being "inwardly perplexed" (v. 17 AMP), had heard the Spirit speak to him. In obedience, he followed. He mentioned the difficulty of his position and concluded, "But God has shown me that I should not call any person common or unclean" (v. 28 ESV). Peter then stood up and said, "I now realize how true it is that God does not show favoritism but accepts from every nation the one who fears him and does what is right" (v. 34–35). This graphic encounter surely lies behind the great statement of the borderless Christ of Saint Paul: "There is neither Jew nor Gentile, neither slave nor free, nor is there male and female, for you are all one in Christ Jesus" (Galatians 3:28).

Here, at the start of the life of the church, is a clear and powerful example of how we are called to behave around people of different backgrounds, cultures, languages, religions, and lifestyles. This liberating story should guide us each day when we encounter the inevitable differences of the workplace. God created all the people we live and work with; he loves each one of them and calls us to respect them while remaining firm in our calling to serve him alone as we demonstrate his love to others.

At Pentecost, people started speaking in other languages (Acts 2:4). Languages are closed universes except to those who understand.

To the outsider, any foreign language is gibberish. But in one act, the Spirit broke linguistic borders, and people spoke to and were understood by others in their own tongues.

Those around them were perplexed: "How is it that we hear, each of us in his own native language? Parthians and Medes and Elamites and residents of Mesopotamia . . . we hear them telling in our own tongues the mighty works of God" (vv. 8–11 ESV). The great genius of Pentecost was that they could understand the truth that was being spoken in the languages with which they were most familiar.

This moment at Pentecost was a supernatural breaking of usual linguistic borders—and a highly unusual event. However, the Spirit can still help us today to break through the barriers of language and culture to reach others with a sensitivity and discernment born of God. If we are truly to fulfill our callings in the world—both generally, to make the good news of Jesus known, and individually, to pursue his calling for our own lives—then we need to be able to reach people in their vernaculars. We need Spirit-inspired words, not dry and dusty "religious" language. Our words must recognize our common humanity to find intimacy and shared understanding with people from all walks of life.

This was made clear to me when I recently took a non-Christian friend to an evangelistic talk. In truth, the talk didn't do much for me, and I left feeling disheartened that my efforts to share the gospel seemed to have been wasted. But when I asked my friend how he had found it, he was buzzing with excitement about what he had just heard! I pushed him to find out why he had liked the speaker so much: "Because he spoke my language," my friend replied.

As Paul said in his letter to the Corinthians, "I have become all things to all people so that by all possible means I might save some" (1 Corinthians 9:22). This is a great work of the Spirit—to help us engage across cultural and linguistic borders. But it also requires some effort on our part to meet people where they are and not simply where we would like them to be.

This new paradigm of the Spirit also brings with it a new *proprietary* regime. The old borders of property, ownership, and competition have been broken. In Acts 4, we learn that the early Christians held their property in common (v. 32). In their very nature, proprietary rights are restrictive, personal, and for the benefit of the owner. And it is right that this should be so. But the Spirit broke these borders in order to allow radical common sharing to the point that "there was not a needy person among them" (v. 34 ESV). I am always inspired by those many Christians who open the doors of their homes and share their time with the lost, the needy, and the poor. As Christians, we should always be open to sharing our food, our shelters, or our financial resources with others.

I remember the wife of a pastor telling me that, growing up, she always used to have tea after school with her close friend, whose family was Christian. Their door was always open to her; they made her so welcome in their home. She never heard them once preach the gospel, but she recognizes her gradual conversion to Christ during that season of spending time in her friend's home.

A wise Christian told me that the best test to shift a mind-set from owning to sharing was "use it or lose it." If you have an asset, share it, or the blessing will simply become a burden.

A certain kind of freedom comes from sharing. The early followers of Jesus did not enforce a communist regime whereby everything was owned and controlled centrally. The Spirit's call is not dictatorial but discretionary. He leaves it to us how we deal with our assets, but we will always be called to share what we have.

The Spirit of God does not only break down the human barriers of culture and language, however. In his power, the Spirit of God is also able to break the borders between the normal and the supernatural, traversing the physical laws of nature. At Pentecost, the physical laws were broken. There was a "mighty rushing wind" (Acts 2:2 ESV) and "tongues of fire that separated and came to rest on each of them" (v. 3). The Holy Spirit, who heralds the empowering presence of the Father, can do so without physical constraint. If nothing else, this event is a reminder that God is supernatural and sovereign and can act as he will, not just within the limitations of our own worldviews and expectations.

So when Peter stooped to talk to a beggar in Acts 3, he knew that physical restrictions no longer limited the work of the Spirit. With a new authority, Peter said, "'In the name of Jesus Christ of Nazareth, walk.' Taking him by the right hand, he helped him up, and instantly the man's feet and ankles became strong. He jumped to his feet and began to walk" (vv. 6–8). Today, the same Holy Spirit still empowers us to see the proclamation of the word accompanied by signs and wonders.

BREAKING FREE

God's Spirit also breaks down the borders that lie within us. Our life callings are not confined to preset outcomes. Paul wrote to the Corinthians, "Where the Spirit of the Lord is, there is freedom" (2 Corinthians 3:17). Freedom comes from breaking down the barriers within our own lives: our personal histories, our childhood traumas, our lack of forgiveness, our self-limitations and misunderstandings. I think of the phrase from the Nigerian poet Ben Okri, who spoke of "the bullies that our pasts have become."[2] Many of us know that sense of being trapped in a distressing pattern of shame we seem unable to break. The tragedy is that these memories become real barriers to fulfilling our true callings. But by his grace, the Spirit of God breaks these patterns and enables us to live lives that are filled with the love of Jesus Christ—and so we are empowered and set free to live out our callings more effectively.

God longs for us to live in wide-open spaces unshackled by inhibitions from the past.

We remember again Paul's words: "Your lives aren't small, but you're living them in a small way." We remember his invitation:

"Open up your lives. Live openly and expansively!" (2 Corinthians 6:11–13 THE MESSAGE). This is what we aspire to.

The problem for so many of us is how to break out of a pattern of conformity. I recall a colleague who had grown up with the expectations from his parents that he would be a banker; his life had been predicated on the fact that banking would be his calling. We worked together for some time before it became clear that he would not make it. And yet he could hardly face family and friends, as the assumption was that he was meant for finance. Sadly, those who had these views of him never actually asked him what his real passion in life was. If they had, they would have known that he was devoted to wildlife conservation. Others' words and expectations can be damaging, but the Spirit of God has the power to enter the darkest shadows of our souls, where these words lurk, and shine his light onto them, defusing their power.

Finally, my colleague broke through the wall and went to spend three years working with rhinos in Tanzania, where he was blissfully happy. Since then, he has never looked back, and the barriers that held him back, once broken, released him to a career in wildlife management, where his financial skills have actually been put to good use.

I think of the hesitant entrepreneur, Will, who came to see me wanting to start a new business. The comfort of his regularly paid job was assuring, but he aspired to more. It was hard to break through the psychological and practical barriers that held him back: the monthly income, the regular hours, the familiar faces, the established working environment. These obstacles were not without their merit, but they were borders the Spirit wanted him to break.

We prayed and we talked and, above all, we tried to imagine the advantages of breaking out of conformity to a certain pattern—the pattern of life in a large, structured company. Will started to wonder if it was in fact more "him" to be entrepreneurial, to break out of corporate life. But he still had nagging questions. So I told him a story from my own life about a rhino named Tsholompe.

Tsholompe was a young calf that lived in a large, fenced wilderness area in South Africa. From a young age, he was a difficult and naughty calf who always tried to break through the fences. After every attempt, a helicopter had to be dispatched, at serious expense, with a trained vet who would dart Tsholompe with a tranquilizer and bring him back to his own area. The fence had to be repaired and the ever-patient neighbor assuaged with a libation of one sort or another. There was much discussion at the broken fence on how to deal with the nonconforming rhino.

Tsholompe's name in the African dialect is translated as "one who causes grief to his parents"—he certainly did to his mother! White rhino calves run behind their mothers, as opposed to black rhino calves, who run in front. His mother clocked him and was constantly giving a backward look at the ever-playful but somewhat uncontrollable Tsholompe.

Tsholompe was born wild. He wanted to roam freely, and he did not accept the imposed borders of the land registry. Whenever he tried an escape, it was always greeted with shaking of heads by the African staff muttering, "Tsholompe does not like to be hemmed in."

Sadly, the story doesn't have a happy ending. Tsholompe lived many happy years in total disobedience, until one evening he fell over during one of his breakouts. Unable to right himself, he was caught in a freezing *vlei*, an African swamp. Every effort to revive him with heat and blankets, and even intravenous fluids, failed.

There is a bit of Tsholompe within all of us. Not that we are meant to live lives of lawlessness, riding roughshod over social boundaries as Tsholompe so often did, but that there is something within us that yearns for the freedom God promises. We are not meant to be hemmed in. We are called to roam freely without the borders of social or peer pressure. Jesus kept the law but broke the rules—a good model for us.

Tsholompe's story seemed to work for Will. He took the risk and started a media business with a friend. The Spirit of God emboldened them and has led them in new directions they could not have imagined while they were living within the structures of their previous jobs.

In many ways, the story of Tsholompe is a parable for all of us. So often we try to conform to patterns that were never intended to be ours. There are times when we just want to break loose. Often these are moments inspired by the Spirit, encouraging the breaking down of previously inhibiting ways of thinking and acting. The Holy Spirit transforms us by the renewing of our minds and we, like Will, see his good, pleasing, and perfect will.

THE CLOTHING OF THE SPIRIT

What does all this mean for our callings?

Everything.

It is the Spirit who makes our callings known, who gives us confidence, and who empowers us to break down the barriers that impede our way. Apart from the Spirit, our lives remain empty.

I have been deeply challenged by the life of Gideon. He grew from a very low point—defensive and lacking in self-esteem—to someone who recognized God's empowering call on his life, broke out of his defensive mentality, and overcame the seemingly impregnable barriers that he faced.

We find the story of Gideon in Judges 6. The setting is a familiar one. The Israelites had turned from the Lord and from his protection only to find themselves confronted by enemies far greater and stronger than they were. This time the nomadic tribes of Midian were their oppressors. For years, the Midianites had terrorized the people of Israel to such an extent that they had retreated to caves, clefts, and gated communities. The Israelites tried to carry on with their lives—they tilled fields, planted crops, and watered green shoots—but whenever the harvest came, the Midianites descended like a swarm of locusts to attack and steal the fruit of the Israelites' labors.

Into this defensive scene came Gideon, in verse 11, threshing wheat in a winepress. Through the years of oppression, Gideon tried to eke out an existence. That he was threshing in a winepress is deeply significant. Threshing was normally done on a hilltop, where the wind can blow the chaff away from the wheat. A winepress, by contrast, was small and enclosed. Gideon was hiding away indoors, away from the sight of the Midianites, who were bent on stealing whatever they saw. He was doing the right thing but in the wrong place.

While Gideon was at work, hiding away and minding his own business, afraid and alone, the Lord called out to him. (It's worth remembering that God speaks to us even at work!)

"The LORD is with you, mighty warrior" (v. 12).

The salutation of the angel of the Lord was as ironic as it was brutal. "Mighty warrior" is in fact the English translation of Gideon's Hebrew name, but at that moment Gideon had probably never felt less like a mighty warrior in all his life. He had been driven back by the relentless pursuit of the Midianites. Years of repressed anger welled up within him. I suspect that he was hurt deeply by the reminder of his name. He probably saw himself as a wimp and not a warrior.

"If the LORD is with us, why has all this happened to us? Where are all his wonders that our ancestors told us about when they said, 'Did not the LORD bring us up out of Egypt?' But now the LORD has abandoned us and given us into the hand of Midian" (v. 13).

Gideon was afraid and angry. Like a cornered animal, he lashed out, venting his frustration and anger at the apparent emptiness of God's promises. But the angel's words were reassuring. God was with him. God was sending him and would go with him.

To this reassurance, Gideon protested: "How can I save Israel?

My clan is the weakest in Manasseh, and I am the least in my family" (v. 15). But the Lord insisted. "I will be with you" (v. 16).

In that short exchange Gideon realized he was loved. God had recognized him, and there can be no greater sign of love than being recognized for who we are. Gideon was known. The Lord called him by name—not only by his given name but by the name of the person that he was going to become. God has great interest not just in who we are now but in who we will become by his Spirit. And Gideon was *called*. He was given the task of delivering the nation from the ravages of the Midianites.

While studying this passage, I was struck by one of the most important features in our calling as Christians: the source of our confidence. We will never be able to connect with other people if we are not connected to ourselves. And we will never truly connect with ourselves unless we are connected to God. The first lesson that Gideon had to learn was to be connected to himself.

Gideon had so withdrawn from the life around him that he had forgotten who he was. He had forgotten his true identity in God, and he needed to be awakened to his true worth. In all callings, the first task of the Spirit is to prepare us to receive his promises. Often we are so weighed down that we struggle to receive from him. Gideon's first step was to accept that he was indeed a mighty warrior, however inhibited he must have felt secretly threshing away in the winepress, constantly at the mercy of the Midianites. It was from this moment of connection that Gideon grew into his calling. It was not an instantaneous event but a gradual move into God's will.

Here is the cornerstone of our callings. When we become secure in our identities, we become less threatened, less defensive, and more open to being the people we are called to be. It is then that we find the inner freedom that gives us confidence to take the initiative, to be bold, to take risks, and to make courageous choices. This is the great work of the Spirit of God. Here we see those internal borders being broken.

The angel of the Lord's commission to Gideon was this: "Go in the strength you have and save Israel out of Midian's hand" (v. 14).

"The strength you have" is the crucial phrase. The angel of the Lord was telling Gideon that what he had was enough. His strength was enough, for, as Paul would remind the Corinthians hundreds of years later, God's "power is made perfect in weakness" (2 Corinthians 12:9).

The Spirit of the Lord says the same to us today. Our hopes, our dreams, our passions, and our strengths are enough for God. His Spirit can take what little we have and use it for his purposes. He will show us where we are called, if only we let him.

So it was with Gideon. He recognized in his encounter with the Lord a call to holiness. He had to clear out the stuff that was displeasing to God, and it started at home, as Gideon went to cut down the idols of his father's house (Judges 6:25–27). When God liberates us into our true identities, our first acts will always be to get rid of the idols—greed, money, selfishness. Before any of our callings can be pursued, we need to have tidied up our own backyards from the idols that have been allowed to grow unchallenged.

Gideon was now in touch with his God and with his inner self. He was confident in his identity. The next stage was for him to be empowered. Verse 34 tells us that Gideon was filled with the spirit. A literal translation is that the Holy Spirit clothed himself in Gideon. It is an extraordinary image—the Spirit of the living God actually wrapping himself in the very identity of this newly connected Gideon, a person connected to God and now empowered by the Spirit of God. We will never fulfill any aspect of our callings unless we allow ourselves to be clothed by the Spirit of God.

It was here that Gideon famously laid a fleece before God, asking him to first make the fleece wet and ground dry, and then the ground dry and the fleece wet. We often interpret this passage as Gideon putting God to the test. We think that Gideon was asking God to prove himself, before Gideon would do what he asked.

When we look closely at the text, however, we see that this isn't the order in which events proceed.

At this point in the narrative, the Spirit of the Lord had already clothed Gideon, who called an army together in order to march toward the Midianites. Gideon already knew what he had to do. His fleece was not a condition of his loyalty to God or of his willingness to follow through on God's commands.

What Gideon wanted from God was not proof on which to base a decision, but proof that God's promise of support still held true. "If you will save Israel by my hand as you have promised" (v. 36) is not a condition but a request for confirmation. Gideon knew that without God this attack would fail, but with God at their backs the Israelites had nothing to fear. In humble and faltering words, he simply requested a sign from God that would give him confidence in battle.

"Do not put the Lord your God to the test" (Luke 4:12) is an important lesson of the Scriptures. But there is nothing wrong with asking God to build our confidence. After all, as Jesus said, "how much more will your Father in heaven give good gifts to those who ask him!" (Matthew 7:11).

THE CONFIDENCE OF GIDEON

Gideon's confidence continued to grow. He had been called, he had been clothed with the Spirit, and he had received confirmation of the Lord's support. There was one more process to go through before his confidence was fully established. He had to rely on God's plans rather than his own.

Gideon assembled a large army to march against the Midianites. This was not God's plan. Gideon's confidence would lead him to believe that he, rather than God, would have fulfilled his calling. God therefore told Gideon to cull his army. From an army of thirty-two thousand, he sent home ten thousand who were filled with fear.

Then there is a second culling. Gideon was urged to cut the

numbers by watching the way in which the remainder drank water. Those who lapped water like dogs were chosen over those who didn't. Of the thirty-two thousand, only three hundred now remained. He now had less than 1 percent of the original army.

We want to be among that 1 percent. It is not enough simply to be confident in ourselves; we need to be called, clothed, and culled. We need to have all the support structures on which we would rely tested before we can see our callings flourish. Often we are reliant on our own insights, power, skills, and confidence, when God wants to show us a better way of trust in Jesus.

The second culling is often the hardest. To let go of everything on which we rely, believing that God will equip us for life's challenges better than we could ever equip ourselves—that takes some doing.

We need this preparation. Otherwise we will try to beat whatever opposition we face with the weapons of our enemy. And we won't prevail. We are called to fight the good fight with the armor of God, not the weapons of the world. To take on the challenges of engaging the world, standing up for what is true, showing compassion for the weak and the marginalized, working toward flourishing employees in our places of work.

Gideon was now ready for battle. He was ready to fulfill his calling. With limited resources and utterly dependent on God, Gideon instructed the three hundred to break into groups of one hundred. He gave them trumpets to carry in one hand and torches covered with clay pots to carry in the other. They were without any offensive weapons, but they encircled the Midianite army. Gideon commanded his men to sound the trumpets and to break the coverings over their torches. In that moment he gave them a war cry: "A sword for the LORD and for Gideon" (Judges 7:20).

I have been overwhelmed by this cry. It sounds right: to him be the glory! But that is not what the text says. Gideon the wimp had now become the warrior, so convinced was he of his identity in God. He was now at the peak of his confidence—identity and destiny fused together. No longer was he filled with self-loathing, ashamed and angry at the sound of his own name. Now he proclaimed it with a Spirit-given confidence that he could never have imagined possible. Gone were his anger and his protestations. Now he accepted himself to the point that his name became the rallying call and not the retreat. He was utterly reliant on God to fulfill his calling. What he would never have been able to achieve in his weakest moments, lacking confidence in himself and in his future, he was now able to achieve. There was no holding back.

The enemy was routed and the people of God were freed.

Gideon is an everyman. Like many of us, he doubted everything about himself, thinking that he had come from the smallest family in the smallest tribe from one of the smallest nations. He could not believe his calling until he grew into the confidence that God gives to those who are obedient. There is power in the Spirit of God to transform every individual and to allow each one of us to believe that, in his power, we will become the people God intended us to be.

BEAT YOUR BENCHMARK

We all have comfort zones, spaces within which we feel safe to operate. But we know that we will never be able to achieve our callings if we operate only within those structures. We learn from Gideon that however weak we may feel, we are strongest when we draw comfort from our special relationship with God. We are strongest when we confront the borders of our comfort zones in the power of the Spirit of God and push the perimeters in search of the wide-open spaces that God has for our lives.

Let me end with a challenge to beat your benchmark.

The 1968 Olympics were famous for being the first televised games. US athlete Bob Beamon was competing in the long jump. He wanted to attempt to break the record at the time, which stood at 27 feet, 4.75 inches.

There was silence around the stadium as Beamon prepared to jump. For a full twenty minutes afterward, the crowd waited in suspense. The measuring equipment was electronic for the first time, but it was not calibrated to cover a jump of this distance. When the results were finally given, Beamon collapsed on the ground, unable to believe what he had achieved. He had jumped 29 feet, 2.5 inches (just under 9 meters!), nearly two feet farther than the previous record.[3] He had not simply set out to improve his previous best by a few inches, but to do the very best that he could. He wanted to make the most of his years of skill as a long-jump athlete. It was one of the greatest moments in Olympic history.

When the Holy Spirit breaks down the borders in our lives, we can achieve extraordinary things. Sometimes, as in the case of Beamon, we don't instantly know the result. God gives us faith to persevere during the waiting. As with Beamon, all we need to do is use to the best of our abilities what God has given us, and he will take care of the rest.

Several years ago, an enormous financial crisis loomed in Europe. The very survival of the structure of the euro currency, if not the whole of Europe, was at stake.

All eyes were on one man: the head of the European Central Bank.

Financial markets and currencies plunged all through the morning, and the only question on anyone's lips was, "What will he say?" His words would either cause an implosion or the reversion of the volatility.

On the morning of July 26, 2012, he stood up, and when asked what he would do to protect the euro, he answered in three simple words.

"Whatever it takes."

At that moment, in human terms, he spoke for the might of the major industrial countries of Europe. As soon as he spoke those words, the markets rallied. The immediate crisis was over. The structure of the currency was secured.

There's a challenge here for us.

When confronted with a world in need of the gospel of Jesus Christ, with a world crying out in pain, with a world riven by inequality, poverty, and need, how will we respond?

Will we hunker down in our winepresses and ignore the outside world? Will we refuse to listen to the still small voice of God gently beckoning us out of our caves and into the light? Will we keep our lamps hidden in jars of clay?

Or will we be willing to say, "Whatever it takes"?

Whatever it takes to see our communities restored, our workplaces transformed, our world healed?

Whatever it takes to see justice and righteousness roll on like a river?

Whatever it takes to see our friends, colleagues, and neighbors come to realize that they, too, are known, loved, and called by their Father in heaven?

God is not calling someone else. He's calling *you*. Calling you to join him in the transforming work of the kingdom of God.

God knows you. He knows who you have been, and he knows who you are becoming. He knows what you have is enough for the plans he has in store for you.

God loves you. He has seen your darkest moments and your greatest triumphs, and he has loved you just the same.

And God calls you. He has called you out of darkness and into the light. And now he calls you to spread that light wherever your feet may carry you.

There is no power on earth equal to the power of forgiven men and women who are known, loved, and called by Jesus Christ.

My prayer, for myself and for you, is that we might have the confidence to step into our callings and journey with God. For I know that if we do, that journey will be the greatest adventure we could ever imagine.

ACKNOWLEDGMENTS

THIS BOOK BEARS THE FINGERPRINTS OF MANY CONTRIBUTORS. The leadership team at Holy Trinity Brompton, my home church, has been instrumental in shaping my thoughts about the distinctive calling of Christianity, and they have allowed me to test some of these ideas in my preaching there. Particular thanks must go to the two Nickys—Gumbel and Lee—for their insight and wisdom. We have journeyed together for more than forty years since our faiths came alive at university, and they, together with their wives, Pippa and Sila, have been a formative part of my Christian life.

Special thanks must go to my team of *logothanatists* ("word-killers")—Alice Goodwin-Hudson, Tom Andrew, and Jo Glen. I can only hope that some beauty emerges from the brutality they showed in their enthusiasm to kill off my alliterative excesses! I am also indebted to the many people who read and commented on early drafts of this manuscript, especially R. T. Kendall, Rob McDonald, and David Ingall, whose theological reflections helped iron out some of the theological creases in my writing. Needless to say, any heresies that remain are entirely my own.

My thanks go to the publishing team at HarperCollins, particularly David Moberg and all the senior executives who met en masse to hear my first thoughts and who have been such a consistent encouragement. Also to Matt Baugher, Joel Kneedler, and

Meaghan Porter, who have read the manuscript and helped turn it into a better book than it would otherwise have been.

It goes without saying that I owe a great debt of thanks to my family—my wife, Fi, and our children—for their support, encouragement, and endless patience. Similar thanks go to those who have suffered the perjury of endorsing this book—many of whom have played a key role in my own journey with God.

Finally, I want to say a huge thank-you to all those who have contributed to this book unwittingly: those pressing inquirers with searching questions about their life-callings; those late-night gatherers on the roof garden of our house, talking into the early hours about life and its purposes; those new Christians starting out in the life of faith and wondering whether the world can really be enough. It is their questions that I have grappled with in the preceding pages, and it is for them that this book was written.

I wish I could style myself an expert on Christian calling. But as often happens when dealing with the affairs of God, I have perhaps been left with more questions at the end of writing than I started out with at the beginning. The journey of discovering a life-calling is one filled with questions, with wrestling, and with a search for truth. It doesn't come in a neat, systematic package to be carefully unwrapped and assembled like some existential flat-pack bookcase. It is a journey of faith, to be experienced in the day-to-day questioning of a life lived to the full.

Nevertheless, what I have tried to do in these pages is to distill some of my own forty years of experience in business and finance into something practical and applicable in the everyday of our rapidly changing world. I hope that it has given you just a glimpse of the excitement of being loved, known, and called by Jesus Christ.

NOTES

CHAPTER 1: CALLED TO PASSION

1. Rick Warren, *The Purpose Driven Life* (Grand Rapids: Zondervan, 2002), 17.
2. Frederick Buechner, *Wishful Thinking: A Seeker's ABC* (New York: Harper and Row, 1973), 95.
3. Barney Calman, "Fibbing on Facebook Can Trick Your Memory: People Start Believing Their Own Social Media Exaggerations," *Daily Mail*, December 27, 2014, http://www.dailymail.co.uk/health/article-2888454 /Youngsters-airbrushing-reality-social-media-make-lives-interesting -suffer-paranoia-sadness-shame-fail-live-online-image.html.

CHAPTER 2: CALLED TO ENGAGE

1. Immanuel Kant, "Idee zu einer allgemeinen Geschichte in weltbürgerlicher Absicht," *Berlinische Monatsschrift*, November 1784, S. 385–411.
2. LeBron James's Facebook page, September 23, 2015, https://www .facebook.com/LeBron/videos/10153669500753944/.
3. Larry Page, "Where's Google Going Next?" filmed March 19, 2014, TED video and transcript, 23:30, https://www.ted.com/talks/larry _page_where_s_google_going_next/transcript?language=en. (The relevant quote is at 22:00.)
4. Peter Taylor, "Nelson Mandela: Everyone Can Make an 'Imprint' on the World," *One* (blog), July 21, 2009, http://www.one.org /international/blog/nelson-mandela-everyone-can-make-an-imprint

-on-the-world/; "Mandela's Birthday Message," BBC, July 18, 2009, Adobe Flash video, 0:57, http://news.bbc.co.uk/2/hi/africa/8157470 .stm. (The relevant quote is at 0:35.)

5. Hans Küng, *On Being a Christian*, repr. ed. (Garden City, NJ: Image Books, 1986), 231.

CHAPTER 3: CALLED TO FLOURISH

1. "Warren Buffett Invites Joey Prusak, Good Samaritan Dairy Queen Employee, to Shareholders Meeting," *HuffPost Good News*, September 24, 2013, http://www.huffingtonpost.com/2013/09/23 /joey-prusak-warren-buffet-_n_3977043.html.

CHAPTER 4: CALLED TO WAIT

1. Tom Callahan, "The Greatest of Them All: Jackson and Jordan Might Be the Two Best Athletes in America. But Who's Better?" *Newsweek*, December 4, 1989, 92.

2. Gary Mack and David Casstevens, *Mind Gym: An Athlete's Guide to Inner Excellence* (New York: McGraw-Hill, 2001), 15–16.

3. R. Judson Carlberg, "Translating A. J. Gordon's Global Vision into Globalization: A Look Ahead," *Stillpoint*, Fall 2005, 15, http://www .gordon.edu/download/galleries/2005%20Fall%20Stillpoint1.pdf. Italics are the author's emphasis.

4. Rick Weinberg, "53: Johnson Flunks Drug Test, Loses Gold Medal," ESPN, July 17, 2004, http://espn.go.com/espn/espn25/story?page =moments/53.

CHAPTER 5: CALLED TO CHOOSE

1. Augustine, *Confessions*, 9.4.11.

2. William Shakespeare, *Troilus and Cressida*, ed. Barbara A. Mowat and Paul Werstine (New York: Washington Square Press, 2007), 2.2.15–16. References are to act, scene, and line.

3. Steve Jobs, commencement address (transcript), Stanford University, Stanford, CA, June 14, 2005, http://news.stanford.edu/news/2005 /june15/jobs-061505.html.

4. Ibid.

5. Ibid.

CHAPTER 6: CALLED TO COURAGE

1. "I'm Forrest . . . Forrest Gump," *Forrest Gump*, directed by Robert Zemeckis (1994; Los Angeles: Paramount Home Video, 2001), DVD.

2. J. K. Rowling, "The Fringe Benefits of Failure, and the Importance of Imagination" (commencement speech, Harvard University, Cambridge, MA, June 5, 2008), *Harvard Gazette*, http://news.harvard.edu/gazette /story/2008/06/text-of-j-k-rowling-speech/.

3. Ibid.

4. Frank Lewis Dyer and Thomas Commerford Martin, *Edison: His Life and Inventions*, vol. 2 (New York: Harper, 1910), 616.

5. Henri J. M. Nouwen, *The Dance of Life: Weaving Sorrows and Blessings into One Joyful Step*, ed. Michael Ford (Notre Dame, IN: Ave Maria Press, 2005), 202.

6. Richard Branson, *The Virgin Way: Everything I Know about Leadership* (New York: Portfolio, 2014).

7. "Elisha Otis," The Elevator Museum (website), accessed April 18, 2016, http://www.theelevatormuseum.org/e/E-5.htm.

CHAPTER 7: CALLED TO FOCUS

1. James Delingpole, "When Lego Lost Its Head—and How This Toy Story Got Its Happy Ending," *Daily Mail*, December 18, 2009, http:// www.dailymail.co.uk/home/moslive/article-1234465/When-Lego-lost -head—toy-story-got-happy-ending.html.

2. T. S. Eliot, "Burnt Norton," *Four Quartets* (New York: Harcourt, 1943), 17.

3. Ryan Jaslow, "Internet Addiction Changes Brain Similar to Cocaine: Study," CBS News, January 12, 2012, http://www.cbsnews.com/news /internet-addiction-changes-brain-similar-to-cocaine-study/.

4. Anthony Storr, *Jung* (New York: Rutledge, 1991), 102.

5. John Milton, *Samson Agonistes* in *The Complete Poems of John Milton*, Harvard Classics, vol. 4 (New York: P. F. Collier, 1909–14), lines 38–46; Bartleby.com, 2001, http://www.bartleby.com/4/602.html.

6. Isaac Newton to Robert Hooke, February 5, 1675, Simon Gratz collection, 9792, Historical Society of Pennsylvania, http://digitallibrary .hsp.org/index.php/Detail/Object/Show/object_id/9285.

7. Hillsong Live, vocal performance of "Beautiful Exchange," by Joel Houston, June 29, 2010, on *A Beautiful Exchange*, Hillsong, CD.

8. For more information, visit http://www.bibleinoneyear.org.

9. Sam Wells, "God Is With Us," YouTube video, 25:29, from a speech delivered at Focus 2014, Camber Sands, Rye, Kent, August 6, 2014, https://www.youtube.com/watch?v=Ruhx6Gm2l9w.

10. Ian Sample, "Shocking But True: Students Prefer Jolt of Pain to Being Made to Sit and Think," *Guardian*, July 3, 2014, http://www .theguardian.com/science/2014/jul/03/electric-shock-preferable-to -thinking-says-study. The details of the study can be found in Timothy D. Wilson, David A. Reinhard, Erin C. Westgate, Daniel T. Gilbert, Nicole Ellerbeck, Cheryl Hahn, Casey L. Brown, and Adi Shaked, "Just Think: The Challenges of the Engaged Mind," *Science* 345:6192 (July 4, 2014), 75–77.

11. Diarmaid MacCulloch, *Silence—A Christian History* (New York: Penguin, 2013).

CHAPTER 8: CALLED TO PERSEVERE

1. Andrew Bisharat, "Duo Completes First Free Climb of Yosemite's Dawn Wall, Making History," *National Geographic*, January 14, 2015, http:// news.nationalgeographic.com/2015/01/150114-climbing-yosemite -caldwell-jorgeson-capitan/.

2. Stav Ziv, "Yosemite Climbers Find Themselves on Top of the World," *Newsweek*, January 19, 2015, http://www.newsweek.com/yosemite -climbers-find-themselves-top-world-300581.

3. Kevin Jorgeson, Instagram post, January 7, 2015, https://www .instagram.com/p/xkK2Z7pm0Y/.

4. Ziv, "Yosemite Climbers."

5. Scot Murray, "The Joy of Six: Sir Alex Ferguson," *Guardian*, November 4, 2011, http://www.theguardian.com/sport/2011/nov/04 /joy-of-six-sir-alex-ferguson.

6. Tommy Caldwell, "Tommy Caldwell: What I've Learned," *Rock and Ice* 217 (April 2014), http://www.rockandice.com/lates-news/what-ive -learned-tommy-caldwell.

7. Hillsong Live, vocal performance of "Mighty to Save," by Ben Fielding and Reuben Morgan, March 5, 2006, on *Mighty to Save*, Hillsong Australia, CD.

CHAPTER 9: CALLED TO WORSHIP

1. Samuel Taylor Coleridge, *The Rime of the Ancient Mariner* (1834), in *The Oxford Book of English Verse, 1250–1900*, ed. A. T. Quiller Couch (Oxford, Clarendon, 1919), lines 283–86, 289–92; Bartleby.com, 1999, http://www.bartleby.com/101/549.html.

2. Karl Barth, "The Gift of Freedom: Foundation of Evangelical Ethics," in *The Humanity of God*, trans. Thomas Wieser (Louisville: Westminster John Knox, 1960), 78–81.

CHAPTER 10: CALLED TO BREAK BORDERS

1. Hillsong United, vocal performance of "Oceans (Where Feet May Fail)," by Matt Crocker, Joel Houston, and Salomon Ligthelm, February 22, 2013, on *Zion*, Hillsong Sparrow, CD.

2. Ben Okri, *Mental Fight: An Anti-Spell for the Twenty-first Century* (London: Phoenix House, 1999), 9.

3. Larry Schwartz, "Beamon Made Sport's Greatest Leap," ESPN.com, accessed April 18, 2016, https://espn.go.com/sportscentury/features /00014092.html.

About the Author

Born and raised in South Africa, Ken Costa studied law and philosophy at college in Johannesburg, where he was actively involved in the student protest movement against racial segregation in universities. In 1974 he moved to England to study law and theology at Cambridge University before joining the investment bank SG Warburg in the City of London. Over the next forty years, Ken continued to work in investment banking, becoming chairman of Europe, the Middle East, and Africa for UBS Investment Bank and later chairman of Lazard International. During this time Ken worked in mergers and acquisitions, advising global corporations on their international strategies, and in 2010 he played a key role in the sale of Harrods—perhaps the most famous department store in the world. In 2016, he was nominated as one of the City of London's top deal advisors of the last twenty years. His first book, *God at Work*, drew on this experience to explore what it means to live every day with purpose in the workplace. Ken also went on to make a series of short films called *God at Work Conversations*, which can be found at **www.godatwork.org.uk/conversations**.

Besides his commercial work, Ken has spent much of his adult life involved in the leadership of Holy Trinity Brompton (HTB), the largest Anglican church in the United Kingdom, where he preaches regularly. He is dean of the HTB Leadership College London, which trains those in their twenties and thirties to be distinctive

Christian leaders in their workplaces, and is also chairman of Alpha International—an evangelistic course born out of HTB, which has so far taught the basics of Christianity to an estimated 27 million people worldwide. He is chairman of Worship Central, a movement promoting worship events and courses across the globe. It was also at Cambridge that Ken got to know the current archbishop of Canterbury, Justin Welby, whose reconciliation and evangelism work he now supports as chairman of the Lambeth Trust.

Given his professional experience, Ken has regularly been asked to speak on financial, ethical, and Christian issues at conferences and churches around the world. As emeritus professor of commerce at Gresham College London, he lectured on finance and ethics in the aftermath of the global financial crisis, and in 2011 he led the London Connection—an initiative seeking to encourage dialogue between the financiers in the City of London and the Occupy protesters who took up residence outside St Paul's Cathedral—at the request of the bishop of London. He was also a trustee of the Nelson Mandela UK Children's Fund for more than ten years, is currently fundraising patron for Great Ormond Street Children's Hospital, and was an advisory board member of the London Symphony Orchestra.

Ken is married to Dr. Fiona Costa, a classical musician and research fellow at the University of Roehampton, and they have four adult children.

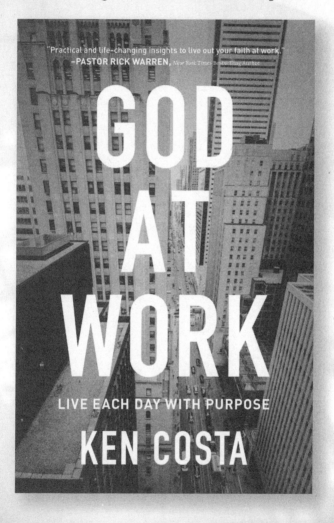